Writing from Within

T0372638

Teacher's Manual

Arlen Gargagliano & Curtis Kelly

CAMBRIDGE
UNIVERSITY PRESS

CAMBRIDGE UNIVERSITY PRESS
Cambridge, New York, Melbourne, Madrid, Cape Town,
Singapore, São Paulo, Delhi, Tokyo, Mexico City

Cambridge University Press
32 Avenue of the Americas, New York, NY 10013–2473, USA

www.cambridge.org
Information on this title: www.cambridge.org/9780521626811

First published 2001
4th printing 2012

Printed in the United States of America
A catalog record for this publication is available from the British Library.

ISBN 978-0-521-62682-8 student's book
ISBN 978-0-521-62681-1 teacher's manual

Telephone numbers, e-mail addresses, and street addresses
given in this book have been created for practice purposes
only and all reasonable care has been taken to avoid using
numbers or addresses that are currently in use. However,
the publisher takes no responsibility for the inadvertent use
of actual numbers or addresses.

Cambridge University Press has no responsibility for
the persistence or accuracy of URLs for external or
third-party Internet Web sites referred to in this publication
and does not guarantee that any content on such
Web sites is, or will remain, accurate or appropriate.

Book design, art direction, and layout services: Adventure House, NYC

Contents

Plan of the book

Writing	Editing	Option
☐ writing a paragraph about things I like to do	☐ paragraph format	☐ writing a paragraph about myself
☐ writing a composition about career choice	☐ sentence connectors	☐ writing a letter requesting information
☐ writing a magazine article about a classmate	☐ direct and indirect speech	☐ writing a resume
☐ writing a composition about an invention	☐ pronouns	☐ writing a letter to a company about a product
☐ writing a composition about an important day	☐ cause-and-effect words	☐ designing a greeting card
☐ writing a guidebook article about a one-day tour	☐ modifiers	☐ writing a letter requesting tourist information
☐ writing a research report	☐ commas	☐ researching restaurants and creating a restaurant guide
☐ writing a magazine article about interviewing techniques	☐ ways of giving advice	☐ reporting on interview results
☐ writing a letter to myself about goals	☐ incomplete sentences	☐ writing about classmates and finding out about myself
☐ writing a composition about dormitory design	☐ articles	☐ designing a dormitory poster
☐ writing a composition about an important person	☐ subject-verb agreement	☐ writing a letter to someone who has influenced me
☐ writing a newspaper article	☐ other words for *said*	☐ writing a letter to my teacher

We, the authors of *Writing from Within*, believe that the greatest hurdle our student writers must face is learning how to organize their writing. Therefore, the main focus of this text is teaching them how to generate topics, write cohesive paragraphs, and organize them into clear, logical expository compositions. We focus on expository writing – or explaining – because it uses an organizational style that differs from the styles used in other languages, and also because it represents the kind of writing our learners will have to do in academic and business environments.

We also believe that excellence in student writing goes beyond mere accuracy or the ability to mimic models. Excellence comes from writing that leads to discovery of self, of ideas, and of others, and self-expression is its own reward. Students should be pulled into learning through interesting and expressive activities rather than be pushed into learning through fear of failure. Therefore, we have chosen to offer writing topics that will challenge your learners' creativity, lead them to introspection, and most important, allow them to experience writing as a joyful exertion.

The focus of each unit is a writing assignment. Some are introspective: For example, learners are asked to reflect on a major life event that has led to growth. Others are more conventional but task-based: Learners are asked to plan a trip abroad and to publish a class newspaper. In this way, humanistic writing assignments are interleaved with task-based writing assignments, providing a broad range of writing experiences. In addition, each unit ends with an optional expansion activity that gives each learner an opportunity to communicate with an outside party.

Each unit offers learners different organizational tools, which are practiced in prewriting exercises. Learners are trained in using a variety of expository modes, such as Division, Classification, and Cause and Effect. Editing skills are taught by giving learners practice in mechanics and grammar. Each unit takes 3–5 hours of class time to complete, and although the syllabus is developmental, it is not necessary to do each unit in order.

The Teacher's Manual is designed to give helpful information on using the textbook and adjusting it to suit your particular needs. We suggest you take the time to look over the Student's Book. You can then familiarize yourself with the style and themes of the book.

Writing is a skill. We tell our students that learning to write is like learning to play a musical instrument; the more they practice, the better they will be. *Writing from Within* is designed to demonstrate to learners that they have the knowledge within themselves to develop this skill. We hope they will enjoy this text and we look forward to hearing your comments.

Arlen Gargagliano
Curtis Kelly

How should I use the Teacher's Manual?

Each unit in the Teacher's Manual is about six pages long. It is divided into four sections: 1) a short **Overview** that tells you what the students will do and learn; 2) a Table of contents with the lesson focus and the expected times to complete each lesson; 3) a list of **Key points** – things to keep in mind; and 4) detailed Instructions for each lesson. If you are new at teaching writing and need help, use all four sections. Experienced teachers need only read the first three sections, which together are one page long.

What is the basic organization of a unit in the Student's Book?

At the center of each unit (with the exception of Unit 1) is a composition assignment. The lessons that come before the composition assignment are prewriting activities, in which students generate content and organize it. The lessons that come after the writing assignment are revision, feedback, and expansion activities.

Prewriting
Brainstorming: The topic is introduced and writing ideas are generated.
Paragraph analysis: Students analyze a model paragraph.
Organizational practice: Students learn expository organizational skills and learn how to organize their composition.

Writing
Model and assignment: Students analyze a model and receive instructions for writing their composition.

Postwriting
Editing: Students correct grammatical errors common to beginning writers and edit their composition.
Giving feedback: Students exchange compositions with other students for review and feedback.
Option: Almost a separate unit in itself, the optional writing activity helps students transfer their newly gained skills to a real communicative writing task.

How is Unit 1 different?

In every unit, the students are assigned a multiparagraph composition. In Unit 1, however, they are taught how to write single expository paragraphs. As part of this training, they practice separating general from specific ideas (representing topics and supporting details) and practice writing topic sentences.

Why should students write topic sentences and underline them?

Interestingly, according to research, only a quarter of all published paragraphs actually contain topic sentences. Topic sentences are, nonetheless, a powerful teaching tool. In order to write a topic sentence, the student must know what the main idea of the paragraph is, which research shows exists in all paragraphs. By asking students to underline their topic sentences, teachers can evaluate the coherence and cohesion of the paragraph, and identify the intended organization of a composition at a glance. We recommend you use this technique.

What are some other ways I can teach organization?

First, have your students master the use of transition words. Transition words provide the framework by which the rest of a paragraph is organized. Transition words such as *First, Second,* or *Third* are used to introduce a series of subtopics. *For example* or *In one case* are used to add details. *However* or *On the other hand* are used to show a differing idea or subtopic. *In conclusion* or *Therefore* are used to show an inference or summary. Transition words hold the ideas in a paragraph together and delineate their hierarchy.

Second, concentrate on getting your students to write good introductory paragraphs. Unlike some other languages, English tends to be top-heavy, with the main idea usually introduced at the beginning and then developed through subtopics after that.

Third, give your students practice using the different ways expository writing is organized. These expository writing modes include Process, Logical Division, Comparison and Contrast, Cause and Effect, Definition, Example, and so on. The paragraph analysis models introduce these different ways of organizing, as is explained in the By the way sidebars.

Finally, have your students practice using some of the other tools provided, such as outlining, writing a conclusion, linking sentences, and using paragraph transitions. These are presented throughout the text.

How is English organization different from that of other languages?

Descriptive and narrative writing use spatial and chronological organization, so these types of writing are similar in all languages. Expository and persuasive writing are not. The style of organization used for these types of writing is language specific, and is influenced by the different ways cultures value logic, intuition, and assertion. *Writing from Within* offers more expository writing than persuasive writing, because this is the most common type of writing used at school, at work, and on the Internet.

So what are some of the features of English expository organization? First, it is usually (but not always) top-oriented, with a main idea given at the beginning and every following statement either adding to that idea or introducing another idea on the same level. Second, English is topically organized. Each paragraph has a single topic, and all its contents should be a part of that topic. Third, English expository writing tends toward logic and assertion. It tends to be less personal, less intuitive, more linear, and more declarative than most other languages.

What part of the writing process should I focus on, and how should I correct my students' papers?

If teaching organization is your main goal, then spend more time on prewriting activities. If accuracy is your goal, then spend more time on revision and editing activities. We recommend that you set organization as your main goal, since research shows that this writing skill is so important. Many teachers tend to set accuracy as their goal and engage in extensive error correction, but other research suggests that correction is usually ineffective. It seems only to have an impact when the corrections are made on the syntactic structures the learners are in the process of acquiring, and when the learners have an opportunity to work with the corrections.

If you teach large classes, error correction might not even be an option, so we suggest you only correct organizational errors, such as poor topic sentences or inadequate introductory paragraphs. If you do correct errors, you may wish to devise a system whereby you correct only one kind of error in each

composition, such as those related to the syntactic structure presented in the editing lesson. Even so, it is better to simply mark the errors and have the students correct them themselves.

What does the peer feedback activity (after the editing lesson) do?

Peer feedback is not the same as peer correction, and yet it achieves some of the same goals. Peer feedback gives the learners contact with models written by their peers and strengthens their ability to evaluate writing. When comments from peers go back to the authors, on the strengths and weaknesses of their writing the authors are getting feedback that sheds light directly on their ability to communicate and organize. Of even greater importance, though, is that peer feedback makes students aware that they are writing for a greater audience than the instructor alone.

What are the optional writing activities at the end of each unit?

The final lesson in each unit is an optional second writing assignment. In almost every case, the writing assignment is less rigorous, but will result in written communication with an outside party. These activities help students transfer their newly gained skills to real-world communication. They can be skipped if time is limited.

How can I deal with mixed levels of students in the same class?

Because the writing activities are open-ended, allowing the students to write at their level of competence, mixed levels should not be much of a problem. In some of the more closed-ended exercises, however, grouping students of the same level together might work better for your class, or it may be that grouping students of different levels works better. Whether you should mix or separate students of different levels depends on a number of factors, including learning styles, culture, and classroom dynamics. Experiment.

A greater problem might exist with some students finishing an activity before the others and being left with nothing to do. Keep in mind that it is not necessary for every student to answer every question for learning to occur, and the "compare answers with a partner" option at the end of many exercises exists, in part, to help alleviate this problem.

What if I don't want to do certain lessons?

The Key points section of the Teacher's Manual indicates the minimum set of lessons that must be completed in order to write the composition. The minimum sets contain only three or four of the unit's lessons. Likewise, the units themselves can be skipped or done in a different order. Just be sure that you teach your students how to write paragraphs with topic sentences before you start Unit 2, and teach them how to write introductory and concluding paragraphs before you start units in the second half of the book.

How often should I give homework?

This depends entirely on how your class is scheduled and the type of students you are teaching. The book is set up so that most of the activities can be done as homework.

How should I grade/assess student writing?

Again, the grading system you employ should reflect your teaching goals and the grading standards set by your school. A number of possibilities exist. In addition to features such as homework completion and attendance, you will probably also evaluate compositions. You can grade all of the compositions and ask students to keep them in portfolios, or you can grade only some, by having students write them in class, as tests. You can assign grades by merely rating the organizational features, such as topic sentences, paragraphs, introductions, and overall content, or you can rate accuracy or rhetorical quality as well.

Writing from Within

Teacher's Manual

Preview

Overview

This unit introduces students to the concept and key parts of a paragraph, as well as to the philosophy of *Writing from Within*.

1

- Read the instructions for Exercise 1 aloud.
- Have students work in pairs for three to five minutes to answer the question.
- Walk around the classroom, helping students as necessary.
- Call on pairs to tell you what they've written. Write their answers on the board.

2

- Read the instructions for Exercise 2 aloud.
- Call on a student to read the definition on the bottom of page 3 aloud.

3

- Read the instructions for Exercise 3 aloud.
- Have students read the paragraphs individually. Then call on students to read each paragraph aloud.
- Read the beginning of a aloud, and have students circle the answer they think is better organized, before they read the correct answer.
- Call on a student to read b. Ask students to circle the topic.
- Have students work with a partner to complete c and d.

- Go over answers as a whole class.
- Have students read the letter on page 3 individually.
- Call on individual students to read the letter aloud, paragraph by paragraph.

Answers
3. a. Movies
   b. why I like movies
   c. There are three reasons why I love movies.
   d. Second, Finally

Optional activity

My goal

Write the sentence *My goal in this class is to _____ because I want to _____ .* on the board. Ask students to take a few minutes to finish the sentence. Then ask individual students to state their goals aloud.

Overview

As an introductory unit, this unit has no major writing activity. It familiarizes students with the basic components they will find in the units that follow. Not all the lessons need to be completed, so the unit can be tailored to the particular needs of your students.

This unit introduces the basic structure of an expository paragraph. Students will learn how to organize a paragraph around one main idea and support it.

	Lesson	Focus	Estimated Time
1	What is brainstorming?	Brainstorming	15–20 minutes
2	Main ideas	Analyzing paragraphs	25–30 minutes
3	General and specific information	Learning about organization	25–30 minutes
4	Topic sentences	Learning about organization	20–25 minutes
5	General and specific information	Prewriting	20–25 minutes
6	Things I like to do	Writing	30–40 minutes
7	Paragraph format	Editing	20–25 minutes
8	What do you think?	Giving feedback	25–40 minutes
	Option: Just for fun		45–50 minutes

Key points

➤ This unit is different from the other units. It is a series of independent exercises on organizing paragraphs. The units that follow will be composed of interdependent exercises that support a major writing assignment.

➤ Time can be greatly reduced if the lessons are assigned as homework activities and class time is used for checking the answers.

➤ Sections can be skipped. A minimal set of lessons might include Lessons 4, 6, and 8.

➤ Concentrate on getting your students to understand topic sentences. Although not all real paragraphs actually have them, they are a powerful teaching tool and will be used throughout the book.

➤ If your students do not know each other, we suggest you do not skip the optional "Just for fun" activity. It will help to build student relationships.

- Draw a brain and a storm cloud on the board.
- Tell students that "to brainstorm" means "to write new ideas quickly."
- Call on a student to read the explanation at the top of page 4.
- Say, *Let's brainstorm together*. Write *New York* on the board. Ask, *What does New York make you think of?*
- Write a few words as examples, such as *tall buildings, exciting,* and *great museums.* Then call on students to give you more words. Write them on the board.

1

- Copy the list from Exercise 1 on the board. Then read the instructions aloud.
- Write on the board: *of animals*
  – dogs in the park
  – my cat Mimi
  – zoo animals
- Call on individual students to give examples for the subtopic *of people.* Add their ideas to the list on the board.

2

- Read the instructions for Exercise 2 aloud.
- Have students read the *Things I like to do* list aloud.
- Give students a couple of minutes to add more ideas. Elicit ideas from students.

3

- Read the instructions for Exercise 3 aloud.
- Have students brainstorm for three minutes.
- Walk around the classroom. Encourage students and give them new vocabulary as necessary.

4

- Read the instructions for Exercise 4 aloud.
- Divide the class into pairs.
- Have students compare answers and add more information to their list.

Optional activity

Class favorites
Ask students about their answers. Find out what the class favorites are, and make a chart with the answers. This can also be done as a group activity.

1

- Write the words *Main Idea* on the board. Tell students that in most paragraphs, each sentence is connected to the main idea.
- Have students read the paragraph individually.
- Call on students to read the paragraph aloud, sentence by sentence.
- Have students answer a–c individually. Walk around the classroom to encourage and help students.

Answers
1. **a.** the worries I have (answers will vary slightly)

   b. There are many things that worry me, but the most common ones are being on time, getting my homework done, and saving money.

c. I worry about being on time because I don't want to miss anything.

I worry about getting my homework done because I work and don't get home until late so I don't have enough time to do a good job.

I worry about saving money because I am trying to save money to go to England this summer and now I am spending a lot.

2

- Have students compare answers with a partner.
- Elicit answers from students.

page 7

| Lesson 3 | General and specific information |

Learning about organization

- Have students read the example at the top of page 7 aloud.
- On the board, write:

General Information   *Specific Information*

animals ⟶

colors ⟶

music ⟶

- Call on students to give you specific information, such as *horse, green,* and *classical music,* to complete the chart on the board.

1

- Have students read the charts in Exercise 1 aloud. Explain vocabulary if necessary.

Optional activity

Be more specific!
Ask students to add additional specific information to the charts in Exercise 1.

2

- Read the instructions for Exercise 2 aloud.
- Have students do the exercise individually.
- Go over answers as a whole class.

Optional activity

What's the main idea?
Give groups of students copies of paragraphs taken from their reading skills textbooks. Each paragraph should have a different main idea. Have students read the paragraphs to find the main ideas, and discuss their answers with the group. Elicit answers from students.

Answers
2. a. S action dramas
    S sitcoms
    G good shows on TV
    S news programs
  b. G popular software
    S word-processing software
    S spreadsheet software
    S Internet software
  c. S learning about another culture
    G good reasons to have an international pen pal
    S improving your English writing skills
    S making a friend abroad

3

- Read the instructions for Exercise 3 aloud.
- Have students do the exercise individually.
- Walk around the classroom, helping students as necessary.

4 ───────────────────────────

- Have students compare answers with a partner.
- Go over answers as a whole class.

Lesson 4　Topic sentences

Learning about organization

page 8

- Write the words *Topic Sentences* on the board.
- Read the explanation at the top of page 8 aloud.
- Ask students to look back at the paragraph on page 6 and find the topic sentence.
- Elicit the answer: *There are many things that worry me, but the most common ones are being on time, getting my homework done, and saving money.*

1 ───────────────────────────

- Have students read the paragraphs in Exercise 1, and mark the best topic sentences with a **T**.

2 ───────────────────────────

- Read the instructions for Exercise 2 aloud.
- Have students compare answers with a partner.

3 ───────────────────────────

- Read the instructions for Exercise 3 aloud. Explain concluding statement (the final statement in a paragraph).
- In pairs, have students mark the other sentences in Exercise 1.
- Go over answers as a whole class.

Lesson 5 — General and specific information

page 9

Prewriting

1

- Read the instructions and example at the top of page 9 aloud.
- Write another example on the board, such as:
  G games I enjoy watching
  S the Osaka Tigers
  S World Cup soccer
  S volleyball at the park
- Do not erase the board. You will use the chart again in Exercise 2.
- Have students look at their brainstorming lists from page 5 and underline three items of general information. Have them write the general and specific information in the chart on page 9.
- Walk around the classroom, helping students as necessary.

2

- Read the instructions and example for Exercise 2 aloud.
- Ask a student to give you a topic sentence for the example you wrote in Exercise 1, such as, *There are some sports I enjoy watching*.
- Write the topic sentence the student gives you on the board.
- Have students complete Exercise 2 individually.
- Walk around and check students' books to be sure they understand. Help them if necessary.

3

- Read the instructions for Exercise 3 aloud.
- Have students circle the letter of the sentence they will use to write a paragraph about in Lesson 6.

Lesson 6 — Things I like to do

page 10

Writing

1

- Have individual students read the paragraph aloud, sentence by sentence.
- Have students complete a–c.

> *Answers*
> **I. a.** places I like
> **b.** Near my apartment, there are three places I like to go.
> **c.** Thai Orchid Restaurant, Powell's Bookstore, the park

2

- Have students compare answers with a partner.
- Go over answers as a whole class.

3

- Have students write their own paragraph. Remind them to underline the topic sentence.
- Walk around the classroom, helping students as necessary.

Lesson 7 — Paragraph format

page 11

Editing

- Explain to students that paragraphs in English have a particular shape.
- Call on a student to read one of the paragraphs at the top of page 11.

1

- Read the instructions for Exercise 1 aloud.
- Have students rewrite the paragraphs.
- Walk around the classroom, helping students as necessary.

2 _____

░ Have students compare answers with a partner.

3 _____

░ Read the instructions for Exercise 3 aloud.

░ Have students check the paragraph they wrote in Lesson 6. Students who made mistakes in paragraph format should rewrite their paragraph.

| Lesson 8 | **What do you think?** |

Giving feedback

page 12

I _____

░ Put students into pairs.

░ Tell students that they are going to check each other's paragraph, and that they will need a sheet of paper for Exercise 2.

░ Have students exchange paragraphs. Then read the instructions and questions for Exercise 1 aloud.

░ Have students complete a–e individually. Walk around the classroom, helping students as necessary.

░ When they finish, tell students to exchange books and review their partner's answers. They can then go on to Exercise 2.

2 _____

░ Read the instructions for Exercise 2 aloud. Then call on different students to read the two example notes.

░ Have students write notes to their partner like the ones in the examples.

3 _____

░ Have students exchange notes with their partner.

| Option | **Just for fun** |

page 13

I _____

░ Tell students they are going to do a fun activity that will help them get to know each other better.

░ Read the instructions for Exercise 1 aloud. Ask students for ideas for additional paragraph topics, such as *foods I like to eat, things I like to collect*, and *movies I like to see*.

░ Walk around the classroom and help students as they are writing their paragraph. Be sure they use correct paragraph form.

2 _____

░ Have students follow the instructions for Exercise 2.

░ Collect all the papers, number them, and hang them up around the room. Be sure to keep your own list indicating who wrote which paper.

░ Divide the students into groups of eight if the class is large.

3 _____

░ Read the instructions for Exercise 3 aloud.

░ Have students walk around the room reading the posted papers. Tell students to write who they think wrote each paper in the chart.

4 _____

░ Tell the students who wrote each paper.

░ Call on individual students to find out how many they got correct.

Optional activity

Read it aloud
Select some students to read their paragraph aloud.

Overview

In this unit, students will write a composition in which they suggest possible careers for each other based on personal styles. To gain support for their career suggestions, students will interview each other on their work styles and fill in a chart that shows what job areas their partners are best suited for.

This unit introduces the basic structure of an expository composition. It builds on the ideas introduced in Unit 1. Students will learn how to use a topic sentence and how to organize a paragraph around one main idea. The organizational mode of Logical Division is also introduced.

	Lesson	Focus	Estimated Time
1	Personality and work preferences	Brainstorming	15–25 minutes
2	Organizing ideas logically	Analyzing paragraphs	20–30 minutes
3	Inference sentences	Learning about organization	20–30 minutes
4	Personality interview	Prewriting	15–20 minutes
5	Job placement chart	Prewriting	15–20 minutes
6	A career choice	Writing	45–55 minutes
7	Connecting sentences	Editing	20–30 minutes
8	What do you think?	Giving feedback	30–40 minutes
	Option: Just for fun		60–90 minutes

Key points

➤ In this unit students will learn how to organize paragraphs into a simple expository composition.

➤ The interview and analysis in Lessons 4 and 5 are critical to the success of the unit. You should examine them in detail before class.

➤ Concentrate on getting your students to understand the organization of the basic paragraph, especially topic sentences and the importance of support.

➤ Sections can be skipped. A minimal set of lessons might include Lessons 4, 5, and 6. You can also save time by assigning lessons as homework.

Personality and work preferences

page 14

Brainstorming

1

- Refer to page 4 of this Teacher's Manual for an explanation of *brainstorming* as needed.
- If you have already explained what brainstorming is, write the following headings on the board: *Things I like* and *Things I dislike*.
- Ask, *What are some things that you like? What are some things you dislike?*
- Call on students to give examples for either category.
- Have students brainstorm for three to six minutes to complete the lists.
- Walk around the classroom to encourage and help students.

2

- Divide the class into pairs.
- Have students compare answers with a partner.

3

- Read the instructions for Exercise 3 aloud.
- Have students write down two possible jobs. Walk around the classroom and help students as necessary.

4

- Have students compare answers with a partner.
- Elicit possible jobs from individual students. Encourage them to tell you why a job is appropriate.

Optional activity

Student survey

Have students, as a whole class, make a questionnaire to ask each other (or another class) which jobs are the most popular. Elicit the results and list the most popular jobs on the board.

Organizing ideas logically

Analyzing paragraphs

page 15

1

- Have students read the paragraph individually.
- Call on students to read the paragraph aloud, sentence by sentence.
- Have a student read the By the way box aloud.
- Have students individually complete a–d. Say, *Remember, the topic introduces the main idea of the paragraph, but the topic sentence is not always the first sentence.*
- Walk around the classroom, helping students as necessary.

Answers

1. a. Understanding the three parts of your "personal style" might help when you decide on a career.

b. having friends or being successful, active or passive, and emotional or logical
c. In conclusion, in addition to thinking about your interests, it is also very important to consider your personality when choosing a career.
d. beginning of a new subtopic: *First, Second, Third*
more specific information on the same subtopic: *For example, For instance*

2

- Have students compare answers with a partner.
- Go over answers as a whole class.

10

page 16

Learning about organization

■ Call on a student to read the definition at the top of page 16 aloud.

1

■ Read the instructions for Exercise 1 aloud.
■ Have students complete a–f individually.

Answers
 1. a. Sandy would make a better scientist than artist.
  b. Being a writer seems like a good career for Akemi.
  c. The job of fashion designer would be perfect for Joe.
  d. A career in sales would suit David.
  e. Mimi seems to prefer physical activities to mental activities.
  f. The job of stockbroker would be ideal for Carol.

2

■ Have students compare answers with a partner.
■ Go over answers as a whole class.

Optional activity

Which is the inference sentence?
In groups, have students write three supporting sentences and one corresponding inference sentence. Then ask them to exchange sentences with another group, and have them figure out which sentence is the inference sentence.

page 17

Prewriting

1

■ Read the instructions for Exercise 1 aloud.
■ Have students work in pairs to complete a and b.

Answers
 1. Answers will vary. Possible answers:
  a. be outside
   use a computer
   meet new people
   travel
  b. convincing people
   planning trips

2

■ Read the instructions for Exercise 2 aloud.
■ Have students take turns with their partner asking and answering the questions as they complete the chart.
■ Explain vocabulary as needed.

Optional activity

Class chart
Draw the chart on page 17 (without the words) on the board. Elicit responses about what the class prefers for each of the nine pairs of personal characteristics. Ask for a show of hands for each and mark the chart accordingly. Tally the results for your class profile.

Job placement chart

page 18   **Prewriting**

1

▨ Read the instructions for Exercise 1 aloud.

▨ Go over the example as a whole class.

▨ Have students complete the chart individually. Walk around the classroom, helping students as necessary.

2

▨ Read the instructions for Exercise 2 aloud.

▨ Have students write the job that best suits their partners.

3

▨ Read the instructions for Exercise 3 aloud.

▨ Have students suggest another job for their partner.

▨ Brainstorm various additional jobs as a class, and write them on the board.

Optional activity

Guess!

Say a student's name or ask him or her to stand up. With a show of hands, ask the class to guess which of the four jobs best suits that student. Find out from the student if the class guessed correctly.

Lesson 6 **A career choice**

page 19   **Writing**

1

▨ Read the instructions for Exercise 1 aloud.

▨ Refer to the other job possibilities on the board.

2

▨ Read the instructions for Exercise 2 aloud.

▨ Have students read the composition individually.

▨ Call on students to read the composition aloud.

▨ Select a student to give example answers for a and b.

▨ Write the examples on the board.

Answers
2. Answers will vary. Possible answers:
  a. I think Sarah would make a good chef.
  b. First reason: likes cooking
      Second reason: is creative
      Third reason: is interested in food

3

▨ Write the following examples on the board:

Sarah likes cooking more than anything else.
She is a very creative person.
She's interested in all kinds of food.

▨ Call on students to write topic sentences about their partner.

4

▨ Read the instructions for Exercise 4 aloud.

▨ Instruct students to complete their composition on lined paper. You may want to tell them to skip lines because doing so will make their composition easier to edit later.

▨ Have students complete the composition either in class or at home.

▨ Remind students to underline the topic sentence in each paragraph.

page 20   **Editing**

■ Have students take turns reading the information and examples at the top of page 20 aloud.

■ Read the instructions for Exercise 1 aloud.

■ Call on a student to read the paragraph aloud.

Answers

1. Answers will vary. Possible answers:

Yuki is a hard worker. In addition, she is able to finish her work independently. For example, we had a group project to do in our economics class last year. There were three people in Yuki's group. However, at the end of the first semester, both of her

partners transferred to other schools. As a result, she had to do the project by herself. She worked on it in the morning, at lunchtime, and at night. Most people in that situation would have gone to the teacher and asked for help, but Yuki finished the project by herself. Furthermore, it was one of the best in the class. Yuki does quality work. Therefore, I believe she would make an excellent sales representative.

2

■ Read the instructions for Exercise 2 aloud.

■ Have students revise their own composition.

page 21   **Giving feedback**

1

■ Read the instructions for Exercise 1 aloud.

■ Have students read the composition their partner wrote about them.

■ Have them individually complete a and b. Walk around the classroom, helping students as necessary.

2

■ Read the instructions for Exercise 2 aloud.

■ Call on a student to read the letter aloud.

■ Have a student read the By the way box aloud.

■ Have students write their letter either in class or at home.

page 22

1

■ Ask students if they know someone who does a job they are interested in.

■ Elicit answers from students.

■ Read the instructions and information for Exercise 1 aloud.

■ Have a student read the letter aloud.

■ Have students complete the assignment either in class or at home.

Optional activity

Envelope writing
Have students address their envelopes in class. Be sure the students' names and addresses are in the upper left-hand corner.

2

■ Have students mail their letter. You may want to read the letters before they send them.

Unit 3 A dream come true

Overview

In this unit, students imagine that they are living ten years in the future and that they have become famous for their work. They will each play the role of magazine reporter and interview one another to write magazine articles on their partner's rise to success.

This unit introduces the organizational mode of giving support with examples. Students will learn how to write topic sentences supported by facts and examples. It also introduces direct and indirect speech, and resume writing.

	Lesson	Focus	Estimated Time
1	Success	Brainstorming	15–20 minutes
2	Facts and examples	Analyzing paragraphs	20–30 minutes
3	Supporting sentences	Learning about organization	20–30 minutes
4	Looking back on your life	Prewriting	15–20 minutes
5	How successful are you?	Prewriting	15–20 minutes
6	A magazine article	Writing	50–60 minutes
7	Direct and indirect speech	Editing	20–30 minutes
8	What do you think?	Giving feedback	30–40 minutes
	Option: Just for fun		60–90 minutes

Key points

➤ Encourage students to choose great futures for themselves. Value and encourage every student's view of his or her future.

➤ Preparing students for writing the third paragraph of the composition should be handled with care. If this humanistic component is managed well, it will provide great rewards. Make sure students write about positive, real characteristics of their partners.

➤ Concentrate on getting your students to understand the importance of supporting sentences.

➤ Sections can be skipped. A minimal set of lessons might include Lessons 3, 5, and 6.

page 23

Brainstorming

1

▩ Read the instructions for Exercise 1 aloud.

▩ Refer to page 4 of this Teacher's Manual for an explanation of *brainstorming* as needed.

▩ If you have already explained what brainstorming is, write the following headings on the board: *What I need to do* and *Characteristics I need.*

▩ Say, *What are some things you need to do to be successful? What are some characteristics you need?*

▩ Call on individual students to give examples for either category. Write their examples on the board.

▩ Have students brainstorm for three minutes to complete their lists.

2

▩ Divide the class into pairs.

▩ Have students compare answers with a partner.

3

▩ Read the instructions for Exercise 3 aloud.

▩ Call on individual students to tell you the answers they circled.

Optional activity

Class poll

Ask what characteristics the class thinks are the most important for success. Elicit characteristics and write them on the board. Then ask for a show of hands to see how many students have each characteristic on their lists. Find out which five characteristics are the most important.

---

page 24

Analyzing paragraphs

1

▩ Have students read the paragraph individually.

▩ Call on students to read the paragraph aloud, sentence by sentence.

▩ Have a student read the By the way box aloud.

▩ Have students individually complete steps a–d. Say, *Remember, the topic introduces the main idea of the paragraph, but the topic sentence is not always the first sentence.*

▩ Walk around the classroom, helping students as necessary.

Answers

1. a. To make his dream come true, he spent his life fighting racism and prejudice in the United States. (*Note:* The next sentence is a close second choice.)

b. Answers will vary. Possible answers:

1. He was a pastor who believed in love.

2. His "I Have a Dream" speech is still considered one of the best speeches of the twentieth century.

3. He traveled throughout the South helping African Americans register to vote, and he organized a huge march on Washington, D.C.

c. Consequently, many Americans consider him a great leader.

d. D: ". . . by the color of their skin but by the content of their character."

I: King said that he wanted to change the United States . . .

2

▩ Have students compare answers with a partner.

▩ Go over answers as a whole class.

Learning about organization

page 25

■ Call on a student to read the information at the top of page 25 aloud.

1

■ Read the instructions for Exercise 1 aloud.

■ Have students complete the exercise individually. If students are having difficulty, do the first one together before continuing with the rest of the exercise.

Answers

1. Answers will vary. Possible answers:
Donna Karan is an excellent fashion designer.
She designs good-looking and comfortable clothing.
She understands what women like to wear.

One of the best filmmakers is Steven Spielberg.
He makes films for people of all ages.
His films are fascinating and thought-provoking.

I think the most talented actor is Robert De Niro.
He can act in dramas and comedies equally well.
Many younger actors admire his work.

A very successful person I know is my mother.
She manages to juggle family and work responsibilities.
She is very well liked in our neighborhood.

2

■ Have students compare answers with a partner.

■ Elicit several examples from the students, and write them on the board.

Optional activity

Who am I?
Write the name of famous people on pieces of paper. Attach one paper to each student's back, so he or she can't read it. Tell students to walk around asking other students questions for "support clues." They can ask yes/no questions such as "Am I a famous actor?" or "Do I play baseball?" but not wh- questions such as "What do I do?" or "What sport do I play?" After students have guessed their identities, they can take their paper tag off and help others.

Prewriting

page 26

1

■ Read the instructions for Exercise 1 aloud.

■ Have students answer the first question individually. Walk around the classroom, helping students as necessary.

2

■ Read the instructions for Exercise 2 aloud.

■ Go over the example.

■ Have students complete their own chart. Walk around the classroom, helping students as necessary.

■ Encourage students to be creative and choose great futures for themselves, in which they have become world-famous and have won awards.

Answers

2. Answers will vary. Possible answers:
Today's date: October 15, 2012
What I am today: a famous writer
Year   Key events in my rise to success
2006   graduated from college
2007   worked for the *Washington Post* newspaper

2009	graduated from graduate school in journalism
2009	published my first novel
2010	Won the Pulitzer Prize for a series of articles on the homeless
2011	Moved to Nice, France, and wrote a second book
2012	Worked as French correspondent for *The Times* in London

Optional activity

Interviews
As homework, have students interview friends and family members about their successes. Students can then report on their findings in small groups or as a whole class.

Lesson 5	**How successful are you?**

Prewriting

page 27

1

- Read the instructions for Exercise 1 aloud.
- Read the questions aloud.
- Have students interview their partner. Walk around the classroom to encourage and help students.

Answers
1. Answers will vary. Possible answers:
   Today Momoko is a writer. She has written two novels. She won a Pulitzer Prize for her newspaper articles.

   In 2006, she graduated from college worked for the *Washington Post* and went to graduate school in journalism.
   She published her first novel in 2009 and the next year, won the Pulitzer Prize for a series of articles on the homeless.
   In 2011, she moved to Nice, France, and wrote a second book.
   A year later she began working as the French correspondent to the London *Times*.

Optional activity

Using a thesaurus
Divide the class into groups of three or four. Give each group a thesaurus. Ask the groups to look up some of the characteristics they have used to describe their partners, and write down the synonyms. Then have each group teach the other groups at least one or two words.

2

- Read the instructions for Exercise 2 aloud. Define words as needed.
- Have students complete the exercise individually.
- Walk around the classroom, helping students as necessary.

Answers
Answers will vary. Possible answers:
2. persistent, self-confident

3

- Read the instructions and example for Exercise 3 aloud.
- Have students complete the exercise individually.
- Elicit possible sentences and write them on the board.

Answers
3. Answers will vary. Possible answers:
   I think Momoko became successful because she is persistent and self-confident. She has such strong determination to succeed. For example, even though she had to study for graduate school and take care of her family, she was still able to work on newspaper articles and write books.

1

■ Read the instructions for Exercise 1 aloud.

■ Have students read the composition individually.

■ Call on students to read the composition aloud, paragraph by paragraph.

■ Have students individually complete steps a–c.

■ Go over answers as a whole class.

> *Answers*
> **I. a.** Jun-Ho is the most popular film director alive.
> **b.** Jun has been directing films since he was 18.
> **c.** Jun-Ho has two characteristics that have helped make him a great director.

2

■ Read the instructions for Exercise 2 aloud.

■ Have students complete the exercise individually. Walk around the classroom and help students as necessary.

> *Answers*
> **2.** Answers will vary. Possible answers:
> Paragraph 1:
> Topic sentence: Andrea Fisher is the most talented women's basketball player in the world.
> Facts and examples:
> —led her team to four WNBA (Women's National Basketball Association) playoffs
> —scores high in every game

> Topic sentence: Paragraph 2:
> Andrea has been a big fan of basketball since she was four years old.
> Facts and examples:
> —started going to games before she started elementary school
> —played on teams in junior high and high school before earning a college basketball scholarship
>
> Topic sentence: Paragraph 3:
> There are two main characteristics that helped lead Andrea into a successful career.
> Facts and examples:
> —passionate about her sport
> —a team player

3

■ Have the students write their article.

■ Tell the students to give their article a title and write their name as author.

Note: Having students write about their partner's real strengths is a powerful but slightly risky aspect of this assignment. Monitor their choices of strengths, and ask them to write as much as they can in the third paragraph. Later, when the assignment is completed and revisions have been made, be certain the students see what their partner wrote about them.

4

■ Call on a student to read the Self-editing checklist aloud.

■ Give students between five and ten minutes to review their article and complete the checklist.

page 30 **Editing**

▨ Have students take turns reading the information and examples at the top of page 30.

1 _____

▨ Read the instructions for Exercise 1 aloud.

▨ Call on individual students to read the paragraph aloud.

▨ Have students work in pairs or small groups to complete the exercise. Walk around the classroom, helping students as necessary.

▨ Go over answers as a whole class.

Answers
1. Sally Corlin explains that it's her job to know the tastes of her customers.

She says that she always asks them about their kids, so they see that she's really interested.

Frank Wang claims that it's his favorite place to shop.

He adds that he recommends Sally's to all his friends.

2 _____

▨ Read the instructions for Exercise 2 aloud.

▨ Have students write the two sentences. Walk around the classroom, helping students as necessary.

Answers
2. Answers will vary. Possible answers:
Direct speech: He said, "I've dreamed of being a basketball player for as long as I can remember."

Indirect speech: Andrea says she is thrilled to be on one of the world's best teams.

page 31 **Giving feedback**

1 _____

▨ Read the instructions for Exercise 1 aloud.

▨ Have students exchange their article with their partner.

▨ Have students individually complete a–d. Walk around the classroom, helping students as necessary.

Answers
1. Answers will vary. Possible answers:
  a. article about Andrea written by Jeff
  b. heartwarming topic
  c. because I could understand how Andrea felt
  d. I liked paragraph number three best because Jeff explained how hard Andrea worked to be the best in her field.

2 _____

▨ Read the instructions for Exercise 2 aloud.

▨ Have students write their letter either in class or at home.

Answers
2. Answers will vary. Possible answers:
Dear Jeff,
I read your article about Andrea and thought it was very interesting. I liked the way you described how she became successful. In fact, I thought it was heartwarming to learn that she had spent so much time as a child going to basketball games with her father. Also, I could understand her feelings. I also like sports and sometimes I get teased because I am

better than many of the boys, so I could
sympathize with her feeling uncomfortable.
All in all, I really enjoyed getting to know
about Andrea's climb to success!
Sincerely,
Pam

Optional activity

Article display
Have students write or type a final draft of their article.
If possible, include photographs. Display the articles
around the room or in the hall.

3

- Have students exchange letters with their partner.
- Tell students to write what they learned from the feedback on the bottom of their partner's letter.
- Collect the magazine articles. Have students submit their article with their partner's reaction letter.
- Have each student read the article written about him or her.

Option	Just for fun

page 32

1

- Ask, *Do you know what a resume is?*
- Explain that a resume is an important representation of an individual's skills and experience.
- Call on a student to read the information at the top of page 32 aloud.

2

- Have students read and study the resume format.
- Ask a student how resumes are different in his or her country. Elicit responses from other students.

3

- Have students complete the assignment, either in class or at home.

20

Unit 4 *Invent!*

Overview

In this somewhat playful unit, students invent unusual devices, such as self-washing dishes, and write about them. They must concentrate on describing what the invention is or does and how to use it.

This unit introduces the organizational mode of Definition, and teaches students how to write an attention getter (a first sentence used to attract a reader's attention). In the following units, this concept will be expanded upon to include introductory paragraphs. Writing e-mail letters is also introduced.

	Lesson	Focus	Estimated Time
1	Everyday objects	Brainstorming	15–20 minutes
2	Defining a mystery item	Analyzing paragraphs	20–30 minutes
3	Attention getters	Learning about organization	20–30 minutes
4	Be an inventor	Prewriting	20–30 minutes
5	Describing your invention	Prewriting	15–20 minutes
6	Writing about your invention	Writing	50–60 minutes
7	Avoiding repetition	Editing	20–30 minutes
8	What do you think?	Giving feedback	30–40 minutes
	Option: Just for fun		50–60 minutes

Key points

➤ Encourage students to come up with humorous inventions. Be ready to capitalize on their creativity and engage in entertaining activities.

➤ Be ready to provide additional vocabulary related to using machines (*turn on, knob, button,* etc.)

➤ Make sure students include a picture with their composition.

➤ Sections can be skipped. A minimal set of lessons might include Lessons 4, 5, and 6. You can also save time by assigning lessons as homework.

Brainstorming

page 33

1

▦ Read the instructions for Exercise 1 aloud.

▦ Have students work in pairs for three to six minutes to complete their lists.

▦ Walk around the classroom, helping students as necessary.

▦ Write the following headings on the board:

       Objects   *Uses*

2

▦ Read the instructions for Exercise 2 aloud. Call on individual students for examples.

▦ Write the examples on the board. Develop a list of about ten to fifteen objects.

3

▦ Read the instructions for Exercise 3 aloud.

▦ Give students a couple of minutes to choose the two objects from the list.

Optional activity

Top ten list

Divide the class into small groups. Tell each group to make a list of the top ten most important objects in their lives (1 being the most important, 10 being the least). Elicit answers from students and make a class chart with the results.

Analyzing paragraphs

page 34

1

▦ Have students read the paragraph individually. Allow several minutes, or enough time so that it seems the majority of the class has finished reading.

▦ Call on students to read the paragraph, aloud sentence by sentence.

▦ Have a student read the By the way box aloud.

▦ Have students complete a and b individually. Go over answers.

Answers

1. a. a car

   b. people rub them on the outside with special liquids; inside is sometimes filled with music; some people even put telephones inside; they come in different colors, shapes, and sizes; have windows; four black things on the bottom

2

▦ Read the instructions for Exercise 2 aloud.

▦ Walk around the classroom, helping students as necessary. You may want to assign this exercise as homework.

Answers

2. Answers will vary. Possible answers:
My mystery item: disposable camera

Clues: It is great to have one at a party. It is light and easy to use. It is less expensive than a regular one. It sometimes comes in a protective cardboard box. People enjoy seeing what it makes. You look through it and press a button to record important events.

3

▦ Read the instructions for Exercise 3 aloud.

▦ Call on individual students to read their clues, or have the class work in small groups.

▦ Go over answers as a whole class. Say, *What was the most difficult item to guess? Why?*

Learning about organization

page 35

■ Call on a student to read the explanation at the top of page 35 aloud.

1

■ Read the instructions for Exercise 1 aloud.

■ Call on a student to tell the class the answer.

> **Answer**
> 1. game

2

■ Read the instructions for Exercise 2 aloud.

■ Have students complete the exercise individually or in pairs.

■ If students are having difficulty, review the first one together before continuing with the rest of the exercise.

■ Have students compare answers in pairs or small groups.

■ Go over answers as a whole class.

■ Write some of the most interesting attention getters on the board.

> **Answers**
> 2. Answers will vary. Possible answers:
>   Health: An apple a day keeps the doctor away.
>   Candles: Light can be bright, dim, or soft, but with a candle, it can become romantic too!
>   Recording: These round disks aren't going to disappear!
>   Dogs: There is one kind of friend who will always be happy to see you.
>   A dog can offer you constant companionship, love, and a faithful friendship. (topic sentence)

3

■ Read the instructions for Exercise 3 aloud.

■ Call on individual students to tell the class their attention getter.

> **Answers**
> 3. Answers will vary. Possible answers:
>   Catch a smile and keep it forever (for disposable camera).

Prewriting

page 36

1

■ Read the instructions for Exercise 1 aloud.

■ Have students work in pairs to answer the questions.

■ Go over possible answers as a whole class.

> **Answers**
> 1. Answers will vary. Possible answers:
>   Bathing suits with safety air bags:
>   This could be a life-saving device. They would be used by people who can't swim, or maybe by people who are swimming in areas where there are strong currents. They would be used by children.

Dishes that don't need washing:
   These are used to save time and energy. They would be used by very busy or young people.

Insta-English dictionary ring:
   This would be used to learn English without effort. It would be used by people who have difficulty remembering words, or who are in a hurry to learn English.

2

■ Read the instructions for Exercise 2 aloud.

■ Have students complete their own drawings. Walk around the classroom, helping students as necessary. You may wish to assign this for homework.

Optional activity

Invention show and tell
Have students bring in one item that they believe is an excellent invention. It should be small and easy to carry, such as a corkscrew or an eggbeater. Have students prepare a two-minute talk about the invention, including instructions on how to use it, and why it is such a great device.

Lesson 5	Describing your invention

page 37 **Prewriting**

1

2

■ Read the instructions for Exercises 1 and 2 aloud.

■ Have students complete the two exercises individually. Walk around the classroom and help students as necessary.

■ Be prepared to give additional vocabulary for describing or operating devices, such as:

button	screen	pull
knob	power cable	push
handle	battery	insert
switch	controls	remove
dial	turn on	record
gauge	adjust	focus
instrument panel	rotate	press

Answers
Answers will vary. Possible answers:
1. My invention is a windshield wiper for eyeglasses. It keeps water off the glasses when it's raining. There is also a cleaner option, so that the wearer can clean the lenses. Eyeglass wearers don't have to worry about their vision ever being unclear.
2. First, press the tiny button on the side of the glasses that activates the wipers. The wipers will start moving. Second, press the button again. The cleaning liquid will squirt out. Next, after the glasses are clean, the wipers will turn off automatically. Then, press the button a third time to dry your glasses. Finally, put your glasses on. You will be able to see perfectly.

3

■ Read the instructions for Exercise 3 aloud.

■ Have students work for several minutes with a partner.

4

5

■ Read the instructions for Exercises 4 and 5 aloud.

■ Have students complete the two exercises.

Answers
Answers will vary. Possible answers:
4. The *Wipe-away* cleans eyeglasses automatically.
5. Are you tired of always wiping your eyeglasses?

Optional activity

Making commercials
Have students work in pairs or small groups. Let them choose one of the inventions from Lesson 5 to advertise. Have the group prepare a short commercial in which they introduce and describe the product. Remind them to try to "sell" the product, and introduce advertising vocabulary such as *new, improved,* and *the greatest.* If you have access to a video camera, tape the commercials and play them back for the class to watch.

Writing about your invention

page 38 **Writing**

1

- Read the instructions for Exercise 1 aloud.
- Have students read the composition individually.
- Call on students to read the composition aloud.
- Read the instructions for a–c aloud and have students follow the directions.
- Go over answers as a whole class.

Answers
1. a. attention getter: Do you wish you could speak English better?
   topic sentence: Easy to use and effective, the Insta-English Ring is an excellent aid for English study.
   b. The Insta-English Ring is a special device that gives you English fluency.
   c. The Insta-English Ring is easy to use.

2

- Read the instructions for Exercise 2 aloud.
- Have students complete Exercise 2 individually. Walk around the classroom and help students as needed.

Answers
2. Answers will vary. Possible answers:
   Paragraph 2: The *Wipe-away* is a special tool to help keep your eyeglasses clean and your vision clear.
   Paragraph 3: It is easy to activate the *Wipe-away*.

3

- Read the instructions for Exercise 3 aloud.
- Have students write their composition on a separate piece of lined paper. Tell them to skip lines. You may want to assign the composition as homework.

4

- Call on a student to read the Self-editing checklist aloud.
- Give students about five minutes to review their composition and complete the checklist.

Avoiding repetition

page 39 **Editing**

- Call on individual students to read the information and examples at the top of page 39.

1

- Read the instructions for Exercise 1 aloud.
- Call on individual students to read the paragraph aloud.
- Have students work in pairs or small groups to complete the exercise. Walk around the classroom and help students as necessary.
- Go over answers as a whole class.

Answers
1. Answers will vary. Note that not every *memophone* should be changed to a pronoun. In fact, it is important that several remain. Possible answers:

The **memophone** is a device designed to send short memos. ~~The memophone~~ *It* is a box that plugs right into your telephone. Inside ~~the memophone~~ *this device* is a microphone, computer chip, and mini-fax. As you speak to someone on the telephone, **the memophone** listens to what you say. Anytime you tell someone to do something, ~~the memophone~~ *it* records your words and

sends them as a fax to the other person's
telephone. Thanks to ~~the memophone~~ *this wonderful little machine*,
the other person will receive a written note
to remind him or her what to do.
~~The memophone~~ *It* will keep printing out
the same note every day until that person
pushes ~~the memophone's~~ *its* "Done" button.
~~The memophone~~ *It* also has "Levels of
Importance Sensors," too. If your voice
sounds urgent, **the memophone** will print
the message in red ink instead of black,
and ~~the memophone~~ *it* will send it once an
hour instead of once a day. For example, if
you call your husband and say, "You forgot
to pick up the dry cleaning yesterday.
Please, please, don't forget today!" **the
memophone** will immediately print out a
red memo saying, "Pick up laundry today!"
This time, thanks to ~~the memophone~~ *this helpful device*,
he'll probably remember.

Optional activity

Discussion

Have students discuss the memophone in small groups.

Write the following questions for discussion on the board:

What do you use to remind yourself or others of things that need to get done?

How could the memophone change your life?

What would you use it for?

2

▨ Read the instructions for Exercise 2 aloud.

▨ Have students review the composition they wrote for Lesson 6. You may have students exchange compositions with a partner to edit for repetition.

| Lesson 8 | **What do you think?** |

page 40

Giving feedback

▨ Say, *We're going to work in small groups to review our class inventions.* Divide the class into groups of four.

1

▨ Read the instructions for Exercise 1 aloud. Call on individual students to read a–e.

▨ Have students exchange compositions and complete a and b independently.

▨ Have students work in groups to complete c–d. Walk around the classroom and help as needed.

▨ Read e aloud. Call on a representative from each group to tell the class about the invention that the group chose.

2

▨ Read the instructions for Exercise 2 aloud.

▨ Have students write their letter either in class or at home.

Answers

2. Answers will vary. Possible answer:
Dear Tom,
    I liked your wonderful invention a lot.
However, I have a few questions about it.
Though I really think the windshield
wipers on the eyeglasses are very useful, I
am now thinking of something that might
be even better. Have you ever considered a
defogger? It could be just like the kind we
have in cars. I understand that this
wouldn't help in the rain, but it would
certainly help in temperature changes.
Anyway, I think it would be a wonderful
addition to your invention.
Sincerely,
Jill

3

- Have students return the composition to its author.

- You may want to call on several students to discuss their feedback. Ask students what they learned from their partner's feedback.

Optional activity

Art gallery
Have students write or type a final draft of their composition. Display the compositions and drawings around the classroom or hallway.

Option	Just for fun

page 41

- Say, *We've been working on giving feedback to each other. Now we are going to work on giving feedback to a company.*

1

- Call on a student to read the information in Exercise 1 aloud.

2

- Read the instructions for Exercise 2 aloud.

- Have a student read the e-mail aloud. Explain the sections to the left of the e-mail.

3

- Read the instructions for Exercise 3 aloud.

- Tell students that they will need to choose either a question, a problem, or an appreciation for the content of their letter.

- Have students complete the assignment and send their letters. You may want to proofread the letters before they are sent.

- Have students bring in any responses they receive.

It changed my life!

Overview

In this unit, students are asked to think about major life events that have led to their personal growth. They choose one event to write about in a cause-and-effect composition. They write about what they were like before the event, what happened, and how they changed.

This unit introduces the expository organizational mode of Cause and Effect. It teaches students how to write introductory paragraphs, which are also powerful tools for organizing compositions. In the optional final lesson, they will also write greeting cards.

	Lesson	Focus	Estimated Time
I	An important event	Brainstorming	15–20 minutes
2	Cause and effect	Analyzing paragraphs	15–25 minutes
3	Introductory paragraphs	Learning about organization	20–25 minutes
4	A major life event	Prewriting	15–20 minutes
5	An important day	Writing	20–30 minutes
6	My big event	Writing	50–60 minutes
7	Cause-and-effect words	Editing	15–20 minutes
8	What do you think?	Giving feedback	30–40 minutes
	Option: Just for fun		50–60 minutes

Key points

➤ Make a special effort to create a classroom environment that encourages self-disclosure.

➤ Students may be interested in the wisdom and developmental insights in each other's composition, so you may want to schedule some time for sharing.

➤ Emphasize that introductory paragraphs are excellent tools for organizing writing.

➤ Sections can be skipped. A minimal set of lessons might include Lessons 3, 4, 5, and 6. You can also save time by assigning some lessons as homework.

page 42

Brainstorming

1

- Read the instructions for Exercise 1 aloud.
- Have students brainstorm for three minutes to complete their lists.
- Walk around the classroom and help students as needed.

> *Answers*
> **1.** Answers will vary. Possible answers:
> Important events
> birth of my child
> winning a race
> visiting my pen pal for the first time
> the time my grandfather was sick
> having my teacher visit my home
> getting my puppy
> the time my family went on a vacation
> getting my first job

2

- Read instructions for Exercise 2 aloud.
- Say, *Take a couple of minutes to review your list and decide which events taught you something valuable.*

3

- Read the instructions for Exercise 3 aloud. Review vocabulary as needed.
- Have students work with a partner to complete the exercise.
- Walk around the classroom, helping students as necessary.

> *Answers*
> **3.** Answers will vary. Possible answers:
> Winning a race gave me confidence. I never thought I could run so quickly before. I practiced for weeks. When the day came, I was calm. I just wanted to finish the race – I didn't really care about winning. Then, when I finished, they congratulated me because I came in third place. The ribbon hangs in my room as a reminder that I can do what I set my mind to doing.

Optional activity

Switching partners
Have students change partners and do Exercise 3 again. Tell them that the listening partner should ask at least one question.

page 43

Analyzing paragraphs

1

- Have students read the paragraph individually.
- Call on students to read the paragraph aloud, sentence by sentence.
- Have a student read the By the way box aloud.
- Have students complete a–d on their own. Walk around the classroom and help students as necessary.

> *Answers*
> **1. a.** (1) selfish, (2) fire, (3) lost everything in fire, (4) hard time, (5) new appreciation
> **b.** It's shocking.
> **c.** Although I lost many things in the fire, the experience helped me to grow up.
> **d.** before the fire: Before the fire, I was selfish. I always complained to my mother about how small my room was or how few clothes I had. I never thought about her troubles, just my own.

what happened to the author: Then, the fire came and destroyed everything we owned. We were suddenly poor and we had to borrow everything, even food.

how the event changed the author: At first, I had a hard time, but slowly I began to realize that I didn't really need my old things. I just needed my family. After all, you can get new clothes anytime, but a family can never be replaced. It is true that the fire took many good things from me, but it gave me something, too. It taught me to appreciate people more than things.

| Lesson 3 | **Introductory paragraphs** |

Learning about organization

page 44

■ Call on a student to read the explanation at the top of page 44 aloud.

1

■ Read the instructions for Exercise 1 aloud. Have students read the two paragraphs individually and then complete a–c.

■ Explain vocabulary as needed.

Answers
1. first paragraph:
   a. Today I became an Australian.
   b. Although I originally came here to study for just two years, something terrible happened in my home country that made me decide to stay.
   c. I will tell you about the kind of person I was before this terrible event, what happened, and how it made me decide to call this country my home.

second paragraph:
   a. You've been dreaming about taking a big trip for years, and the time has finally come.
   b. This simple comparison of independent versus group tour travel might change your mind.
   c. It compares cost, safety, and use of time.

2

■ Have students compare answers with a partner.
■ Elicit answers from the students.

2

■ Have students compare answers with a partner.
■ Elicit answers from the students.

page 45   **Prewriting**

1

- Read the instructions for Exercise 1 aloud.
- Allow students a couple of minutes to fill in the three significant events. Tell them that they can add events that weren't initially listed in their brainstorming list.

2
3

- Read the instructions for Exercises 2 and 3 aloud. Have students discuss just one of three topics they listed.
- Allow about 10 minutes for students to complete the two exercises.

4

- Read the instructions for Exercise 4 aloud. You may want to assign this as homework.
- Have students complete the exercise. Walk around the classroom and help as necessary.

Answers
4. Answers will vary. Possible answers:

Before:	After:
selfish	generous
disliked something	began to like it
rich	poor
childish	adult

Optional activity

Memories speaking game
Have students work in small groups. Give each student three index cards. Tell them to write an important life event on one side of each card, and the date it happened on the other side. Have them arrange the cards in chronological order. The student who wrote the earliest date should turn over the card and tell the group about his or her experience. The other students should ask questions to get more information about the event.

page 46   **Writing**

- Read the instructions aloud.
- Have students read the composition individually.
- Call on students to read the composition aloud.
- Have students complete a individually.
- Go over answers as a whole class.
- Read the instructions for b aloud. Have students work independently for several minutes to take notes for their own composition.

Answers
a. attention getter: Have you ever thought that you knew someone very well and then found out that you hardly knew that person at all?
main idea: I thought I knew him well until one day something happened that changed my attitude toward him.
guide: Let me explain how I used to see my father, what happened, and how it changed me.

page 47

Writing

1 _____

2 _____

necessary.

3 _____

- Say, *Now you are going to put your notes together, and write a well-organized composition.*

- Read the instructions for Exercises 1 and 2 aloud.

- Have students write their introductory paragraph.

- Have students write their topic sentences.

- Walk around the classroom, helping students as

- Tell students that they should write their composition on a separate piece of lined paper, skipping lines. You may want to read students' introductory paragraphs before they go on with the composition.

4 _____

- Have a student read the Self-editing checklist aloud.

- Give students about five minutes to review their composition and complete the checklist.

page 48

Editing

- Have individual students take turns reading the information and examples at the top of page 48 aloud.

1 _____

- Read the instructions for Exercise 1 aloud. Emphasize that in some cases the answers will be one sentence, but in other cases, will be two.

- Have students work in pairs to complete the exercise. Walk around the classroom, helping students as necessary.

- Go over answers as a whole class.

Optional activity

Create your own exercise
Have students work in pairs to write an exercise similar to Exercise 1. First, tell them to write five pairs of completed sentences with the cause-and-effect words in parentheses. Then, have each pair of students exchange the sentences with another pair. Write the best examples on the board.

---

2 _____

- Read the instructions for Exercise 2 aloud.

- You may want to have the students show you the changes by underlining the cause-and-effect words.

Answers

1. **b.** The economy is getting worse. Therefore, few companies are hiring workers.
  c. I quit my job because I wanted to become a full-time professional musician.
  d. My father could not walk due to a car accident when he was thirty.
  e. Since my aunt often scolded me, I didn't like her very much.
  f. My sister and I could not agree. As a result, we argued over little things.
  g. My family moved to a foreign country, so I learned a new language.

Giving feedback

page 49

1

■ Say, *We're going to work in small groups to review our compositions.* Divide the class into groups of four.

■ Read the instructions for Exercise 1 aloud. Call on individual students to read a and b.

■ Have each student evaluate one of the other students' compositions.

■ Have groups exchange their compositions and complete c and d individually.

■ Have each group give you their favorite composition.

■ Ask the students with stars on their papers to read their composition to the class. Have students write a Lesson of Life that corresponds with each composition.

2

■ Have students compare their Lessons of Life with a partner.

■ Review the Lessons of Life as a whole class. Write several examples on the board.

Optional activity

Proverbs

Have students make up proverbs based on the events and lessons of life, for example: "Nothing makes you appreciate your family like a fire." Have students write their proverbs in big, clear letters on sheets of colored paper and post them around the classroom.

Option   **Just for fun**

page 50

1

■ Read the questions in Exercise 1 aloud. You may want to bring in a collection of greeting cards to show to students.

2

■ Read Exercise 2 aloud. Write any additional categories on the board.

Answers

2. Answers will vary. Possible answers:
  new baby   sympathy
  going-away   graduation

3

■ Have students evaluate the cards with a partner.

■ Say, *Which card do you like best?* Have the class indicate their favorite by raising their hands. Keep a tally on the board.

4

■ Read the instructions and questions for Exercise 4 aloud. Have students complete a–c.

5

■ Distribute card-making supplies, such as white card stock, markers, construction paper, scissors, and glue.

■ Have students design their card in class. You may prefer to have them design their card at home.

■ Display the finished cards around the class before the students give them away.

Unit 6 *Exciting destinations*

Overview

In this unit, students plan one-day tours to famous resort cities and write guidebook articles about them. In order to do so, they are encouraged to use outside references and write in a guidebook style.

This unit introduces the expository organizational mode of Process. It also trains the students in making suggestions and using more descriptive modifiers in order to write in a guidebook style. In the final lesson they will also learn how to write letters to tour bureaus to request information.

	Lesson	Focus	Estimated Time
1	A recent trip	Brainstorming	10–15 minutes
2	Guidebook style	Analyzing paragraphs	15–25 minutes
3	Making suggestions	Learning about organization	20–25 minutes
4	Researching a famous city	Prewriting	15–20 minutes
5	My itinerary	Prewriting	20–30 minutes
6	A guidebook article	Writing	60–90 minutes
7	Using modifiers	Editing	15–20 minutes
8	What do you think?	Giving feedback	30–40 minutes
	Option: Just for fun		50–60 minutes

Key points

➤ Encourage students to choose locations to write about that they would really like to visit someday. Monitor their choices to reduce redundancy and provide a wide variety of destinations.

➤ Consider grouping students who are working on the same cities, or by geographical area.

➤ Make sure students know how to format a reference and how to include their sources in the final composition.

➤ Sections can be skipped. A minimal set of lessons might include Lessons 4, 5, and 6. You can also save time by assigning some lessons as homework.

page 51

Brainstorming

1

▓ Read the instructions for Exercise 1 aloud.

▓ Have students brainstorm to complete their lists.

▓ Walk around the classroom, helping students as necessary.

2

▓ Read instructions for Exercise 2 aloud.

▓ Say, *Take a couple of minutes to review your list and decide which places and activities were the most memorable.*

3

▓ Read the instructions for Exercise 3 aloud.

▓ Have students compare travel experiences with a partner.

Optional activity

Class tour plans

On the board make two columns under these headings:

| Places I would like to visit | Things I would like to do there |

Elicit ideas from the students to complete the class chart.

page 52

Analyzing paragraphs

1

▓ Read the instructions for Exercise 1 aloud.

▓ Have students read the paragraph individually.

▓ Call on individual students to read the paragraph aloud, sentence by sentence.

▓ Have a student read the By the way box aloud.

▓ Have students individually complete a–d. Walk around the classroom, helping students as necessary.

2

▓ Have students compare answers with a partner.

▓ Go over answers as a whole class.

Optional activity

Scrambled paragraphs

Have students work in small groups. Each group should write a process paragraph using transition time expressions. Give each group enough pre-cut strips of paper to write each sentence of their paragraph on a separate strip, but tell them to leave a blank in place of the time expression. Have each group switch their strips with another group, and try to put the sentences in the original order. They should also guess the missing time expressions and write them in the blanks. When they finish, have them check their results against the original paragraphs.

Answers

1. a. attention getter: Imagine standing under Big Ben or walking through Piccadilly Circus.

   b. topic sentence: To see as much as you can during your visit, you must plan your trip carefully.

   c. subtopics: gather information, make a list, look at a map, write down your travel plans

   d. first, next, after that, finally

Learning about organization

page 53

■ Call on a student to read the examples at the top of page 53 aloud.

1

■ Read the instructions for Exercise 1 aloud.

■ Call on a student to read the example and finish the sentence. Remind students that there are several options.

■ Have students complete a–f individually.

■ Go over answers as a whole class.

Answers

1. Answers will vary. Possible answers:

a. If you go to Paris, you must visit the Louvre.

b. While you're in Tokyo, you should visit Meiji Shrine.

c. While you're in Sydney, you might want to see Bondi Beach.

d. If you go to London, a visit to Buckingham Palace is a must.

e. While you're in Egypt, it's essential that you visit the Pyramids.

---

f. If you go to New York, be sure not to miss Central Park.

g. While you're in Peru, it would be a good idea to visit Machu Picchu.

2

■ Have students write two suggestions. You may want to have them make one strong suggestion and one weaker one.

3

■ Have students compare answers with a partner.

■ Elicit answers from the class.

Optional activity

Recommendation list

Say, What places should we suggest to visitors? *Write a list of places on the board. Then call on students to make sentence suggestions.*

Prewriting

page 54

1

■ Read the instructions for Exercise 1 aloud.

■ Allow students a couple of minutes to look over the map and indicate where they have been or would like to go.

■ Elicit responses from the class. Say, *Where have you been? Where would you like to go?*

■ Write two columns on the board:

Places we've been   *Places we'd like to go*

■ Write students' answers in the columns.

2

■ Read the instructions for Exercise 2 aloud.

■ Give students a few minutes to think about the city they chose.

3

■ Bring in a variety of books and magazines for the students to use as resources.

■ You may choose to send students to the library or to computers to do research. This can be completed in school or at home.

4

■ Read the explanation in Exercise 4 aloud.

5

■ Have students complete Exercise 5.

■ Refer them to the examples in Exercise 4. You may choose to assign this exercise as homework.

page 55   **Prewriting**

▦ Read the instructions at the top of page 55 aloud. Call on students to read the questions.

▦ Elicit possible answers from students.

▦ You may want to model the task first by making an itinerary for your own city. Copy the itinerary chart onto the board. Call on students to help fill it in.

▦ Tell the students to write their own itinerary. Explain that they don't need to write a separate activity for each hour. Three major activities will be enough.

▦ If some students have chosen the same city, you may want to group them together and have them write different itineraries. You might even assign groups of students to the same cities for this purpose.

▦ Walk around the classroom, helping students as necessary.

12:00	Walk to the top of the mountain (about 30 minutes) and have lunch while enjoying a spectacular view of the mountains.
2:00	Visit the Cave and Basin National Historic Site to see the "birthplace" of Banff National Park.
3:00	Go shopping in the little shops on Banff Avenue.
5:00	Go to Banff Upper Hot Springs and bathe in natural hot springs.
8:00	Have dinner at Le Beaujolais, one of the best restaurants in Canada.
10:00	Go back to the Banff Springs Hotel and have a hot chocolate in their beautiful lounge.

Answers

Answers will vary. Possible answer:
Itinerary: Banff, in Alberta, Canada

7:00	Have breakfast at the Banff Springs Hotel and enjoy a great view of the Rocky Mountains.
8:00	Play a round of golf.
11:00	Ride the Sulphur Mountain Gondola – about a 10–15 minute trip on the gondola to the top of Sulphur Mountain.

Optional activity

School tour

Write on the board: *Itinerary.* Ask students to help you write an itinerary for a visitor to your school. Begin with the school's starting time. Elicit suggestions from students and write them on the board. Remind students to use the language for making suggestions they learned in Lesson 3.

pages 56–57   **Writing**

▦ Read the instructions for Exercise 1 aloud.

▦ Have students read the composition individually.

▦ Call on students to read the composition aloud.

▦ Have students complete a and b individually. Walk around the classroom, helping students as necessary.

▦ Go over answers as a whole class.

Answers

1. a. attention getter: Can you visit Las Vegas and not gamble? Absolutely!
   main idea: Here's a one-day tour in which you won't enter a casino even once.
   guide: You'll start the day with a visit to a unique shopping center, then go to a first-class restaurant, and finally end the tour next to a sinking ship.
   b. Answers will vary. Possible answers: visiting the Louvre, eating gourmet food, shopping

2

- Read the instructions for Exercise 2 aloud.
- Have students complete their introductory paragraph in the space provided.

Answers

2. Answers will vary. Possible answers:
You have only one day to see Paris! Where will you go? Our experts will tell you. They suggest you see the world's most famous museum, sample France's delicious gourmet food, and shop for souvenirs or fashionable clothing.

3

- Read the instructions for Exercise 3 aloud.
- Have students write their topic sentences.

4

- Tell students to write their article on a separate piece of lined paper, skipping lines. Walk around the classroom, helping students as necessary.

5

- Have a student read the Self-editing checklist aloud.
- Give students about five minutes to review their composition and complete the checklist.

| Lesson 7 | Using modifiers |

page 58 **Editing**

- Call on a student to read the information and examples at the top of page 58.

1

- Read the instructions for Exercise 1 aloud. Review the vocabulary as needed.
- Have students work with a partner or in small groups to complete the exercise. Walk around the classroom, helping students as necessary.
- Go over answers as a whole class.

Answers

1. Answers will vary. Possible answers:
a. New York City is known for its dramatic skyline.
b. Busy people walk down the bustling streets.
c. Exotic shops in Chinatown sell appetizing foods.
d. Tourists love the breathtaking view from the top of the World Trade Center.
e. Riding New York's affordable subway is an adventure in itself.
f. The exciting nightlife is famous all over the world.

2

- Have students rewrite three sentences from their composition using modifiers.

Optional activity

Using a thesaurus

Obtain several copies of a thesaurus. In groups, have students write the two headings great *and* terrible *on a piece of paper. Then have them use a thesaurus to find ten other words with the same meanings. Tell them to write the words in the columns. Elicit examples from the class and write them on the board. You may want to ask students to use the words in sentences.*

---

page 59

Giving feedback

1

- Read the instructions for Exercise 1 aloud.

- Have students exchange their compositions and complete a and b individually. The group members do not need to agree with one another on their answers.

- Elicit responses from the class.

Answers
Answers will vary. Possible answers:
1. a. Mariko's uses the best guidebook style. She makes Chicago sound very exciting.
   b. I think the Kuala Lumpur tour sounds the most interesting because the food sounds delicious and I'd like to see the world's tallest buildings.

2

- Read the instructions for Exercise 2 aloud.

- Have students complete their postcard individually.

- Have students take turns reading their card.

Answers
2. Answers will vary. Possible answers:
Greetings from New York City!
We've just spent an amazing day in the Big Apple! First we visited the Statue of Liberty. We climbed all the way up. What a view! Then, we went to Ellis Island to see where U.S. immigrants used to first arrive. After that we went to South Street Seaport, where we had a delicious seafood dinner. Tomorrow we're going to some interesting museums. Wish you were here!
Love,
Jane

Optional activity

Tour-agency role play
Group the students by cities in geographical areas. Each group will be a tour agency selling tours to that area. Have them brief each other on their tours, decide prices for each, and make signs or posters for their company. Then set up the tour companies around the classroom. Have half the students run their companies, while the other half act as customers, walking around and signing up for tours. After 15–20 minutes, have them switch roles.

Option | **Just for fun**

page 60

- Have individual students take turns reading the information and examples at the top of page 60.

1

- Read the instructions and questions for Exercise 1 aloud.

- Call on individual students to read the letter.

Answers
1. Hee-Sung lives in San Francisco now. He wants to visit Seattle.

2

- Read the instructions for Exercise 2 aloud. Have students write a rough draft of their letter in class. They should type it or copy it neatly.

- You may want to read the letters before the students send them.

3

- Review proper envelope addressing. Have students address their envelope and send their letter.

- Display any responses that students receive.

Unit 7 Research survey

Overview

In this unit, students conduct simple research on their classmates by choosing a research question and surveying them. The "interviewers" analyze the results by classifying the respondents into groups and then describe these groups and their responses in a composition.

This unit introduces the expository organizational mode of Classification. Students are also taught how to write concluding paragraphs and how to use commas. They will write a restaurant guide in the optional final lesson.

	Lesson	Focus	Estimated Time
1	Getting to know someone	Brainstorming	10–15 minutes
2	Classification	Analyzing paragraphs	15–25 minutes
3	Classifying people or things	Learning about organization	20–25 minutes
4	Concluding paragraphs	Learning about organization	20–25 minutes
5	Class survey	Prewriting	20–30 minutes
6	A research report	Writing	50–60 minutes
7	Using commas	Editing	15–20 minutes
8	What do you think?	Giving feedback	30–40 minutes
	Option: Just for fun		50–60 minutes

Key points

➤ Make sure students choose good research questions to ask their classmates. The questions should be interesting and should lead to a variety of responses, but also allow the respondents to be classified into groups. Questions such as "When is your birthday?" probably will not lead to very interesting compositions.

➤ Emphasize that there are many ways to classify objects into groups and that in choosing a system of classification, the purpose and audience should be taken into consideration.

➤ Point out the importance of concluding paragraphs for giving closure to writing. Three types of conclusions are illustrated here – summaries, predictions, and evaluations – but other types exist as well.

➤ Sections can be skipped. A minimal set of lessons might include Lessons 3, 4, 5, and 6.

page 61   **Brainstorming**

1

- ▤ Read the instructions for Exercise 1 aloud.
- ▤ Have students brainstorm on their own for three minutes to complete their list.
- ▤ Walk around the classroom to encourage and help students.

2

- ▤ Read the instructions for Exercise 2 aloud. Say, *Take a couple of minutes to review your list with your partner and add more items to your own list.*
- ▤ Review the answers as a class by asking students what questions they have on their list. Write the heading *Questions I'd like to ask* on the board, with examples from the students underneath.

Answers
2. Answers will vary. Possible answers:
  How many brothers and sisters do you have?
  Do you have any pets? What kind?
  What do you like to do most in your free time?
  What kind of music do you like?

What do you like to do at night?
What are your plans for the future?
What's your favorite subject in school?
What's your favorite movie?

Optional activity

Scrambled polite questions
Elicit ways to make questions more polite in English. Write these questions on the board. Teach students any of these forms and expressions they don't mention:

May I ask you a personal question? What are your plans for the future?

Could you tell me what your plans are for the future?

Would you mind telling me what your plans are for the future?

Would you mind if I asked you what your plans are for the future?

Stress that word order is different in polite sentences. Then, give students scrambled versions of complete polite questions to put in order. This can be done as a group race.

Analyzing paragraphs
page 62

1

- ▤ Have students read the paragraph individually. Allow several minutes, or enough time so that it seems the majority of the class has finished reading.
- ▤ Call on students to read the paragraph aloud, sentence by sentence.
- ▤ Have a student read the By the way box aloud.
- ▤ Have students complete a–d individually. Walk around the classroom, helping students as necessary.

Answers
1. a. attention getter: How can you find out if you and your spouse are likely to be a good couple?
  b. topic sentence: The psychologist studied married couples to find out how people get along, and she found that there are three types of couples.
  c. subtopics: calm-calm, passionate-passionate, calm-passionate
  d. In contrast – It shows a difference.
    As a result – It shows a conclusion.
    Of course – It shows more information will be added to the previous point.

2

- Have students compare answers with a partner.
- Go over answers as a whole class.

3

- Read the questions aloud and have students discuss their answers with their partner.
- Discuss answers as a whole class.

page 63

| Lesson 3 | **Classifying people or things** |

Learning about organization

- Call on a student to read the explanation at the top of page 63.

1

- Read the instructions for Exercise 1 aloud.
- Have students read the information about the different kinds of fruit.

2

- Read the instructions for Exercise 2 aloud.
- Have students write two more types of classification with a partner.

> **Answers**
> **2.** Answers will vary. Possible answers: by popularity, by size, by shape, by geographic location

3

- Have students work with a partner or in small groups to complete Exercise 3. Remind them that there are many possible answers.
- Go over answers as a whole class.

> **Answers**
> **3.** Answers will vary. Possible answers:
> Audience: cooks
> Groups based on: taste
> Sour: lemons, limes, pineapples
> Sweet: strawberries, grapes, cherries
> Mellow: apples, bananas, papayas
>
> Audience: fashion designers
> Groups based on: colors

Red: apples, cherries, strawberries
Yellow: lemons, pineapples, bananas
Other: grapes, limes, kiwis

Audience: store managers
Groups based on: shelf life
A few days: cherries, strawberries, bananas, grapes
A few weeks: apples, papayas, lemons, limes, pineapples

Audience: shipping companies
Groups based on: durability
Hard to bruise: apples, pineapples
Easy to bruise: lemons, limes, papayas
Very easy to bruise: cherries, strawberries, bananas, grapes

Optional activity

More couple types
Have students make up their own classifications of couples, and conduct an informal survey of what they think the best combination of personality types would be.

Optional activity

Classification
Bring to class a large assortment of international postage stamps or coins. Have students in groups find as many ways as they can to classify the items. After giving them some discussion time, go over each group's categories as a whole class. Some sample classifications for postage stamps might be

stamps with people on them
stamps from Asia
stamps that are in a sheet of stamps
stamps that have been cancelled

Point out to students that there are many ways to classify items and that this is an exercise in creative thinking.

page 64

Learning about organization

- Call on a student to read the information at the top of page 64.

I

- Read the instructions for Exercise 1 aloud. Have students read the concluding paragraphs individually.
- Call on students to read the concluding paragraphs aloud.
- Give students a few minutes to think about and write their answers individually.

Answers
1. paragraph A: summary
paragraph B: evaluation
paragraph C: prediction

2

- Have students work briefly with a partner to discuss their answers, and why they chose them.
- Go over answers as a whole class.

Lesson 5 | **Class survey**

page 65

Prewriting

I

- Read the instructions for Exercise 1 aloud. Call on students to read the questions.
- Have students write their question individually. Be sure they choose a question that will get a variety of responses and that can be classified into groups.

2

- Read the instructions for Exercise 2 aloud.
- Have students write their question and responses on a separate piece of paper. After they begin asking each other questions, walk around and help as necessary.

3

- Read the instructions for Exercise 3 aloud.
- Have students fill out their charts individually. Give them time to analyze the results and help as necessary.
- You may want to have students complete this for homework.

4

- Read the instructions for Exercise 4 aloud. Have students work with a partner for several minutes.
- Elicit answers from the students. Ask for volunteers to share their research questions and responses with the class.

Optional activity

Survey results poster
After students finish their survey, have them make a poster describing the results. Bring in poster board, markers, old magazines, and glue. Encourage students to use charts, graphs, and icons. Put students' posters up in the classroom. After they finish their composition in Lesson 6, students can post their composition next to their poster to serve as an illustration.

pages 66–67 **Writing**

1

- Read the instructions for Exercise 1 aloud.
- Have students read the composition individually.
- Call on students to read the composition aloud.
- Have students complete a–c individually. Walk around the classroom, helping students as necessary.
- Go over answers as a whole class.

> **Answers**
> 1. a. what the writer did: I asked each of my classmates what he or she plans to do after graduating.
>   his or her results: there are three types of students in my class
>   b. second paragraph: Don't Know types
>   third paragraph: Go Back Home types
>   fourth paragraph: Stay Abroad types
>   c. prediction

2

3

- Read the instructions for Exercises 2 and 3 aloud.
- Have students write their topic sentences and concluding paragraph. Monitor and help as necessary.

4

- Have students write their composition on a separate piece of lined paper, skipping lines. You may want to assign this as homework.

5

- Call on a student to read the Self-editing checklist aloud.
- Give students about five minutes to review their composition and complete the checklist.

---

page 68 **Editing**

- Have individual students take turns reading the information and examples at the top of page 68.

1

- Read the instructions for Exercise 1 aloud. Point out the first sentence in which two commas have already been added.
- Have students work individually or with a partner to complete the exercise. Walk around the classroom, helping students as necessary.
- Go over answers as a whole class.

> **Answers**
> 1. Campus fashions might change, but the basic college student is always the same, right? Wrong! College students in universities all over the world have changed a lot in the last thirty years, and we can expect these changes to continue. First of all, whereas college students used to be fairly young, almost all aged between 18 and 22, they are now much older. In the United States, for example, some reports show that there are now more college students older than 22 than younger! In addition, today's students are doing more things than before. Thirty years ago, almost all college students went to school full-time, taking three or more classes. They just studied. Today, however, there are more students going part-time than full-time. They are not just studying. They are studying, working, and raising families. In conclusion, college students are not staying the same – they are changing. In fact, they are changing almost as quickly as campus fashions!

2

- Read the instructions for Exercise 2 aloud. Allow students several minutes to review comma usage in their composition.

Optional activity

More comma practice
Retype a paragraph from a reading book at your students' level, omitting all the commas. Tell students how many commas are missing from the paragraph and have them put the commas in the places they think are appropriate. Check answers as a whole class.

Lesson 8	**What do you think?**

Giving feedback

page 69

1

- Divide the class into pairs.
- Read the instructions for Exercise 1 aloud.
- Have students exchange their compositions and complete a–e independently.

2

- Read the instructions for Exercise 2 aloud. Call on a student to read the letter aloud.
- Have students write their letter individually.
- Have students return the composition, with the letter, to the author.

Optional activity

Giving opinions
Pass out copies of a short news article based on a survey. Have students read the article individually, and discuss their reactions in groups. Elicit responses from the groups to discuss as a whole class.

Option	**Just for fun**

page 70

1

- This restaurant review involves work both inside and outside the classroom. Students are asked to visit restaurants in order to complete their research, but you may choose to do the same activity with theaters, clothing stores, bookstores, or Web sites.
- Ask, *What are the names of some local restaurants?* Have a student write the list on the board.

2

- Divide the class into small groups to choose a restaurant. Make sure the groups all choose different restaurants.

3

- Read the instructions for Exercise 3 aloud.

- Call on a student to read the questionnaire aloud. Give students several days to complete this part of the assignment individually.

4

- Read the instructions for Exercise 4 aloud.
- Have students make notes. Then pass out index cards for the students to write their comments on.

5

- Collect the index cards and compile a restaurant guide.
- Organize the entries by restaurant type or location. Encourage students to add cards as they visit other restaurants.

Overview

In this unit, students will write compositions about how to succeed in job interviews. In order to get information for their compositions, they will discuss interviewing with their classmates, and do "good interview"/"bad interview" role plays.

This unit introduces the expository organizational mode of Comparison and Contrast. Students are trained in using comparative words, and adjusting the strength of a suggestion by using different verbs. They will also talk to experts on job-interviewing techniques in the optional final lesson.

	Lesson	Focus	Estimated Time
1	DOs and DON'Ts of interviews	Brainstorming	10–15 minutes
2	Comparing and contrasting	Analyzing paragraphs	15–25 minutes
3	Expressions that show contrast	Learning about organization	20–25 minutes
4	Interviewing for a job	Prewriting	20–25 minutes
5	Poor interviewing techniques	Prewriting	20–30 minutes
6	Dressing for success	Writing	50–60 minutes
7	Giving advice	Editing	15–20 minutes
8	What do you think?	Giving feedback	30–40 minutes
	Option: Just for fun		50–60 minutes

Key points

➤ If the role plays are set up properly, this unit not only will provide students with information useful to their lives, but will also be rather humorous.

➤ Be sure to define specific jobs for which the students will be writing job interviews.

➤ Make sure students organize the writing for their compositions in a way that leads to comparison and contrast.

➤ Sections can be skipped. A minimal set of lessons might include Lessons 4, 5, and 6. You can also save time by assigning lessons as homework.

page 71

Brainstorming

- Write *DOs* and *DON'Ts* on the board. Ask students if they know what these words mean.
- Explain that in English, when we talk about DOs and DON'Ts, we mean things that we should do and shouldn't do.
- Read the instructions for Exercise 1 aloud.
- Call on a student to read the examples in the book.
- Have students brainstorm individually for three minutes to complete the lists.
- Walk around the classroom to encourage and help students.

> DON'Ts
> look at the clock during the interview
> pretend to know something you don't
> act overly confident
> chew gum
> arrive late

2

- Read the questions and instructions for Exercise 2 aloud. Say, *Take a couple of minutes to review your list and pick your choices for the best and worst thing to do in an interview.*

> *Answers*
> **1.** Answers will vary. Possible answers:
> DOs
> get plenty of sleep the night before
> appear interested and self-assured
> sit up straight
> prepare another copy of your resume
> read about the company beforehand

> *Answers*
> **2.** Answers will vary. Possible answers:
> best thing: appear interested and self-assured
> worst thing: chew gum

3

- Elicit answers from the class. Write each answer on the board in the appropriate column.

Analyzing paragraphs

page 72

- Read the instructions for Exercise 1 aloud.
- Have students read the paragraph individually. Allow several minutes, or enough time so that it seems the majority of the class has finished reading.
- Call on students to read the paragraph aloud, sentence by sentence.
- Have a student read the By the way box aloud.
- Have students complete a–d individually. Walk around the classroom, helping students as necessary.

> *Answers*
> **1. a.** I have two bosses, Michelle and Eliza, and I think Michelle is better.
> **b.** Michelle and Eliza
> **c.** Main idea: two bosses
> Subtopics (may vary slightly): feedback, time, and trust
> **d.** On the other hand – It shows a contrast.
> However – It shows a contrast.
> Furthermore – It shows more information will be added to the previous point.
> In conclusion – It shows a conclusion.

2 _____

- Have students compare answers with a partner.
- Go over answers as a whole class.

| Lesson 3 | **Expressions that show contrast** |

Learning about organization

page 73

- Call on a student to read the information and examples at the top of page 73 aloud.

1 _____

- Read the instructions for Exercise 1 aloud. Warn the students that they may have to add information or write an additional sentence. Call on a student to read the example.
- Have students complete the exercise individually.

Answers
1. Answers will vary. Possible answers:
   b. Eliza never takes the time to talk to me, whereas Michelle always does.
   c. Michelle, unlike Eliza, trusts my decisions.
   d. While Eliza doesn't encourage me very much, Michelle does.
   e. Michelle always keeps her door open. Eliza's, however, is always closed.
   f. I don't like working for Eliza. On the other hand, I love working for Michelle.

2 _____

- Read the instructions for Exercise 2 aloud.
- Have students complete the sentences individually. Walk around the classroom, helping students as necessary.

Answers
2. Answers will vary. Possible answers:
   a. Unlike my best friend, I don't like scary movies.
   b. I'm good at languages. On the other hand, I can't work with numbers at all.
   c. My favorite food is pizza. However, I don't eat it every day.

3 _____

- Have students compare answers with a partner.
- Go over answers as a whole class.

Interviewing for a job

page 74   **Prewriting**

1

▨ Read the directions for Exercise 1 aloud. Give students a few minutes to think about and write their answers.

2

▨ Divide the class into groups of three. Read the instructions for Exercise 2 aloud.

▨ Call on a student to read the sample interviewer's questions.

▨ Have students brainstorm in groups and write down possible questions.

▨ Elicit questions from the class and write them on the board. Don't erase the board because you will use the questions again in Lesson 5. Discuss as a class any questions that may be inappropriate for an interview and erase them from the board.

Answers

2. Answers will vary. Possible answers:
What are some of your long-term goals?
What experience do you have in this position?
What is one thing you have done that you are most proud of?
What is your greatest weakness?

3

▨ Read the instructions for Exercise 3 aloud.

▨ Have students work in their groups to develop a role play. Walk around the classroom to encourage and helps students.

4

▨ After several minutes, have students switch roles and role-play again.

Optional activity

Dream job

Have students write a paragraph about their dream job. Tell them to describe the job in detail. Have them share their paragraph with their group before they do the role play in Lesson 5. The interviewers should tailor their questions to the jobs described in the paragraphs.

Poor interviewing techniques

page 75   **Prewriting**

1

▨ Have students work with the same group they worked with in Lesson 4.

▨ Read the instructions for Exercise 1 aloud. Have students brainstorm a list of inappropriate responses.

▨ Refer to the questions on the board from Lesson 4. Elicit inappropriate responses from students, and write them next to the questions.

2

▨ Read the instructions for Exercise 2 aloud. Tell students to practice interviews with good and inappropriate responses because they're going to perform in front of the class.

3

▨ Read the instructions for Exercise 3 aloud. Call on the different student groups.

▨ Have students in the audience make a list of interviewing DOs and DON'Ts individually.

▨ After each group, elicit from the class the DOs and DON'Ts seen in the role play.

4

▨ Read the question for Exercise 4 aloud.

▨ Call on individual students to state their opinions.

▨ Have students vote on the best interviewee.

1

▨ Read the instructions for Exercise 1 aloud.

▨ Have students read the composition individually.

▨ Call on students to read the composition aloud.

▨ Have students complete a and b individually. Walk around the classroom and help students as necessary.

Answers

1. a. attention getter: My mother used to say, "If you want that job, dress like you already have it."
main idea: First impressions are important, so wearing the right clothes to an interview can make a difference in whether or not you will get the job.
guide: There are three things you must think about when choosing clothes for an interview: color, style, and comfort.

b. second paragraph: The color of your clothes sends a message, so you should fit the clothes to the job.
third paragraph: In addition to color, the style of your suit makes a difference.
fourth paragraph: The last important point about choosing an outfit is whether or not it is comfortable.

2

▨ Read the instructions for Exercise 2 aloud.

▨ Walk around the classroom, helping students as necessary.

3

▨ Read the instructions for Exercise 3 aloud, and have students write their topic sentences individually.

4

▨ Have students write their concluding paragraph.

5

▨ Have students write their composition on a separate piece of lined paper, skipping lines. You may want to assign this as homework.

6

▨ Call on a student to read the Self-editing checklist aloud.

▨ Give students about five minutes to review their composition and complete the checklist.

Optional activity

Dress for success booklet

Bring in (or have students bring in) some fashion magazines for men and women. Have students work in small groups and cut out pictures of clothing they think is suitable or unsuitable for the workplace. Each group should make a booklet describing why the clothes they chose are appropriate or inappropriate.

▨ Call on a student to read the information and examples at the top of page 78 aloud.

1

▨ Read the instructions for Exercise 1 aloud. Read the example.

▨ Have students complete the exercise individually or with a partner. Walk around the classroom, helping students as necessary.

▨ Go over answers as a whole class.

Answers

1. Answers will vary. Possible answers:
b. must not
c. had better/should/ought to
d. had better/should/ought to
e. may not want to

---

f. must
g. had better/should/ought to
h. may want to
i. had better not/shouldn't
j. should
k. must

2

- Read the instructions for Exercise 2 aloud.
- Allow students several minutes to review their composition and complete the exercise.

Lesson 8 | **What do you think?**

Giving
feedback

page 79

1

- Say, *We're going to work in small groups to review our compositions.* Divide the class into groups of four.
- Read the instructions for Exercise 1 aloud.
- Have students exchange their compositions and complete the exercise individually.

2

- Read the instructions for Exercise 2 aloud.
- Have students compare their notes.
- Have students discuss and decide which advice is most useful.
- Have students write the reasons in the paragraph as a group.

3

- Have students report back to the class. Call on individual representatives of the groups to read their paragraphs from Exercise 2.

Optional activity

Interview manual
Choose paragraphs from various compositions written in Lesson 8 to make an interview manual. Select an editing team. Have students design and illustrate the manual as a team. Make photocopies to distribute to the class.

Option | **Just for fun**

page 80

1

- This DOs and DON'Ts activity involves work outside of the classroom. Students are asked to contact two professionals in order to complete this task.
- Read the instructions for Exercise 1 aloud. Have students complete this assignment before the next class.

2

- Read the instructions and example for Exercise 2 aloud.

- Have students look at their completed lists in Exercise 1 and prepare statements individually in both direct and indirect speech.
- Have students meet in groups to report their findings.

3

- Call on student groups to present their suggestions to the class. You may want to have group representatives write the two most interesting suggestions on the board.

Unit 9 — *Personal goals*

Overview

In this unit, students will write a composition about their life goals. In order to get information to write about in their compositions, they will complete two exercises in which they make lists of their future goals.

This unit introduces the concept of the Persuasive mode of expository writing. It also introduces parallel structures, sentence transitions, and run-on sentences.

	Lesson	Focus	Estimated Time
1	In the future	Brainstorming	10–15 minutes
2	Persuasive paragraphs	Analyzing paragraphs	15–25 minutes
3	Parallelism	Learning about organization	20–25 minutes
4	Sentence transitions	Learning about organization	20–25 minutes
5	In my lifetime	Prewriting	20–30 minutes
6	A letter to myself	Writing	50–60 minutes
7	Incomplete sentences	Editing	15–20 minutes
8	What do you think?	Giving feedback	30–40 minutes
	Option: Just for fun		50–60 minutes

Key points

➤ Point out that although they overlap, persuasive writing is different from expository writing. Simply put, *expository writing* means explaining, while *persuasive writing* means convincing.

➤ Make sure the goals that the students set are reasonable, positive, and will require some effort to achieve. However, they should be goals that can be achieved within a few years.

➤ Allow students to modify their goals after seeing those that other students have set.

➤ Make special efforts to maintain a positive classroom environment.

➤ During the final optional lesson, be sure students know that negative comments, even if they are "just joking," will not be tolerated. Tell students that if they can't find anything positive to say to someone they should not write anything.

➤ Sections can be skipped. A minimal set of lessons might include Lessons 5 and 6. You can also save time by assigning lessons as homework.

Lesson 1   In the future

page 81   **Brainstorming**

1

- Write *Changes* and *Future goals* on the board.
- Read the instructions for Exercise 1 aloud.
- Call on a student to read the examples in the book aloud.
- Have students brainstorm individually for three minutes to complete the lists.
- Walk around the classroom to encourage and help students as necessary.

> **Answers**
> **1.** Answers will vary. Possible answers:
> Changes:
> I want to stop putting things off.
> I want to make more time to read.
> Future goals:
> I want to speak Italian fluently.
> I want to live in another country.

2

- Read the instructions for Exercise 2 aloud. Say, *Take a couple of minutes to review your list.*

3

- Ask students if they have any changes or goals in common with their partner.
- Write some examples on the board.

> **Optional activity**
>
> ***Class goal survey***
> *Have students mingle and seek out other students with similar goals. After several minutes, call on students to tell you the goals. Write them on the board for discussion. Allow students to add to their list if they wish.*

> **Optional activity**
>
> ***Future timelines***
> *Have students make a timeline for the next twenty years of their lives. Encourage them to be creative. Have students explain their timelines to each other in small groups, then post the timelines on the classroom walls.*

Lesson 2   Persuasive paragraphs

page 82   **Analyzing paragraphs**

1

- Have students read the paragraph individually. Allow several minutes, or enough time so that it seems the majority of the class has finished reading.
- Call on students to read the paragraph aloud, sentence by sentence. Explain vocabulary as needed.
- Have a student read the By the way box aloud.
- Have students complete a–e individually. Walk around the classroom, helping students as necessary.

> **Answers**
> **1. a.** Life is full of choices.
> **b.** Sometimes by choosing the hardest way, there is more to gain.
> **c.** In short, the easy way isn't always the best way.
> **d.** For example – It introduces an example.
> However – It shows a difference.
> In short – It shows a conclusion.
> **e.** By choosing

2

- Have students compare answers with a partner.
- Go over answers as a whole class.

Optional activity

Mottoes and examples

In small groups, have students write down their personal motto. Have them read their motto to the group, giving two or more examples to support it. Examples may be "Always look on the bright side of life" or "Never give up."

Lesson 3	Parallelism

Learning about organization

page 83

- Call on a student to read the information and examples at the top of page 83 aloud.

- Read the instructions for Exercise 1. Call on a student to read the example aloud.
- Have students complete a–h individually. Tell students to read the whole sentence before making changes.

Answers

1. b. Last night I saw a movie, met some friends, and called my parents.
   c. Penny hopes to finish school, save some money, and start her own business.
   d. Mr. Potter has never seen the ocean, has never been on an airplane, and has never owned a car.

   e. Before you leave, please turn off the lights, water the plants, and lock the door.
   f. Sam McCarthy is a doctor, writer, husband, and father.
   g. The new City Arts Center is modern, functional, and beautiful.
   h. Max was a successful director, a winner of many awards, and an actor.

2

- Have students compare answers with a partner.
- Go over answers as a whole class.

Lesson 4	Sentence transitions

Learning about organization

page 84

- Call on a student to read the explanation and examples at the top of page 84 aloud. Explain that this technique is just one of several that can be used to make smooth transitions.

- Read the instructions for Exercise 1 aloud.
- Call on a student to read the example aloud.
- Have students complete a–h individually. Walk around the classroom, helping students as necessary.

Answers

1. b. October is the best time to visit.
   c. Sean Connery was the most famous.
   d. La Sorbonne in Paris is his first choice.
   e. Hae-won and Peter are the people I am most anxious to see.
   f. World peace is one of the most important.
   g. To send my brother an e-mail message will be my first task.
   h. Spain and Italy are her favorite countries.

2

- Have students compare answers with a partner.
- Go over answers as a whole class.

Optional activity

Make up a new exercise
Have students work in small groups to write a similar exercise for their classmates to complete.

Lesson 5   In my lifetime

page 85   **Prewriting**

1

- You may choose to have students complete Lesson 5 as homework in preparation for the composition they will write in Lesson 6.
- Read the instructions for Exercise 1 aloud. Call on individual students to read the examples given in each category.
- Have students work individually. Walk around the classroom to encourage and help students as necessary.

2

- Read the instructions for Exercise 2 aloud. Allow students several minutes to complete the exercise.
- Remind students that the goals they choose will be used in their composition, so they should be meaningful. Tell them that the deadline does not have to be a date. It can be a year (2012), an age (by 35), or an event (before I get married).

Lesson 6   A letter to myself

pages 86–87   **Writing**

- Have students read the composition individually.
- Call on students to read the composition aloud.
- Have students complete a and b individually.
- Go over answers as a whole class.
- Have students individually write topic sentences for their three goals.

Answers
a. three goals: learn Mandarin, go to China, become more organized
b. second paragraph: First, I want to learn how to speak Mandarin.
third paragraph: Next, I would like to go to China within the next three years.
fourth paragraph: I would like to become more organized.

- Read the instructions for d aloud. Have students write a conclusion for their composition.
- Have students write a letter to themselves. You may want to assign this as homework.
- Call on a student to read the Self-editing checklist aloud.
- Give students about five minutes to review their composition and complete the checklist.
- Read the instructions for g aloud. Encourage students to keep these letters in a safe place until the deadline arrives.
- If you are in a school, you may want to have students choose goals they can complete while they are students. Set the date for opening the letters just before graduation.

page 88

Editing

■ Call on students to read the information and examples at the top of page 88 aloud.

■ Read the instructions for Exercise 1 aloud.

■ Have students work individually or with a partner to rewrite the paragraph. Walk around the classroom, helping students as necessary.

■ Go over answers as a whole class.

Answers

1. Answers will vary. Possible answer:

By the age of forty, I think I will have reached many of my goals because I will have spent so many years working toward them. I will have two children, a boy and a girl. I will be married to a great person, someone who shares my ideas about life and love. We will live in a home full of books instead of televisions, and we will read every night. We'll have some pets, too. Maybe we'll get a dog and a cat. My spouse and I will have good jobs. We'll be able to travel around the world with our children, and sometimes by ourselves if we take time off from our jobs. I think that when I am forty, I will be a happy person.

2

■ Allow students sufficient time to review their composition and complete Exercise 2. You may want to have students highlight any changes they make.

Optional activity

Class reunion

Tell students to imagine that it is twenty years in the future and that the class is going to have a reunion. Teach students some expressions such as

I haven't seen you for so long!
How have you been!
Look at you – you haven't changed a bit!
You look so different – I didn't recognize you!
Tell me what you've been doing!

Let them mingle for at least ten minutes. When the students are finished, ask them what they found out about their classmates.

---

page 89

Giving feedback

■ Say, *We're going to work in small groups to review our compositions.* Divide the class into groups of four.

■ Read the instructions for Exercise 1 aloud.

■ Have students exchange their composition and complete a and b independently.

■ Read the instructions for c aloud. Have students complete c with their group.

2

■ Read the instructions for Exercise 2. Call on a student to read the example.

■ Tell students to write their letter on a separate piece of lined paper, skipping lines. You may want to assign this as homework.

3

■ Have students give their letter to the author.

page 90

1

■ This is an exercise in which all students write one positive sentence about each of their classmates.

■ Arrange the students' chairs in a circle. Have them take out a piece of paper and a pen.

■ Read the instructions for Exercise 1 aloud. Call on students to read a–e.

■ Check that all students understand what they are going to do.

■ Have students pass the papers around until they receive their own paper back.

2

■ Each student will now have a page full of comments about himself or herself. Let students read their paper.

■ You may want to ask students why positive feedback is important. This question can serve as a basis for discussion, or as starter for a short writing assignment.

Unit 10 Architect

Overview

In this unit, students design a college dormitory for international students. They then organize a description of their dormitory and write it in a composition.

This unit introduces the expository organizational mode of Division, also known as Logical Division. The students are also trained in the use of articles. They will make a poster for their dormitory in the final optional lesson.

	Lesson	Focus	Estimated Time
1	Facilities for college students	Brainstorming	10–15 minutes
2	Organizing ideas logically	Analyzing paragraphs	15–25 minutes
3	Dividing topics into subtopics	Learning about organization	20–25 minutes
4	Be an architect!	Prewriting	20–25 minutes
5	A floor plan for a new dormitory	Prewriting	20–30 minutes
6	Dormitory design	Writing	50–60 minutes
7	Using the articles *a*, *an*, and *the*	Editing	15–20 minutes
8	What do you think?	Giving feedback	30–40 minutes
	Option: Just for fun		50–60 minutes

Key points

➤ Make sure the students understand how to use the dormitory floor-plan page in Lesson 5. Show them the model in Lesson 6 beforehand, if necessary.

➤ Encourage students to use colored pencils and let them know that the rooms they include do not have to be shaped exactly like those at the bottom of Lesson 5. They can use curved walls, they can include interior gardens, and they can design the dorm as multiple buildings if they wish.

➤ Spend extra time helping students divide the description of their dorm into subtopics, such as features for "daily living," "study," and "recreation."

➤ Make sure they include the dorm-design floor plan in their composition.

➤ Give them time afterward to look at and discuss other students' designs.

➤ Sections can be skipped. A minimal set of lessons might include Lessons 4, 5, and 6. You can also save time by assigning some lessons as homework.

58

page 91

Brainstorming

1

▨ Write the headings *Buildings, Rooms,* and *Equipment* on the board in three columns.

▨ Read the question and instructions for Exercise 1 aloud.

▨ Have students brainstorm individually for three minutes to complete the three lists. You may want to do the brainstorming activity as a whole class.

▨ Walk around the classroom to encourage and help students as necessary.

▨ Elicit examples from individual students and write them on the board.

Answers

1. Answers will vary. Possible answers:

Buildings:
student center
cafeteria
dormitory
gymnasium

Rooms:
dormitory room
classroom
computer room
kitchen

Equipment:
computer
copy machine
telephone
vending machine

2

▨ Read the instructions for Exercise 2 aloud.

▨ Give students a few minutes to divide their ideas into smaller groups. Walk around the classroom to encourage and help students as necessary.

▨ Say, *There may be some overlap in the function of particular rooms. For example, many people like to study in their dorm room and in the library – or even in the cafeteria.*

Answers

2. Answers will vary. Possible answers:

Rooms for studying:
dormitory
classroom
computer room

Rooms for socializing:
student lounge
dormitory
cafeteria

Rooms for food preparation and eating:
kitchen
cafeteria
dormitory

3

▨ Read the instructions for Exercise 3 aloud. Have students compare lists with a partner.

▨ Go over similarities and differences as a whole class.

page 92

Analyzing paragraphs

1

▨ Read the instructions for Exercise 1 aloud.

▨ Have students read the paragraph individually. Allow several minutes, or enough time that the majority of the class seems to have finished reading.

▨ Call on students to read the paragraph aloud, sentence by sentence. Explain vocabulary as needed.

▨ Have a student read the By the way box aloud.

▨ Have students complete a–d individually. Walk around the classroom, helping students as necessary.

2

- Have students compare answers with a partner.
- Go over answers as a whole class.

Lesson 3	**Dividing topics into subtopics**

Learning about organization

page 93

- Call on a student to read the information and examples at the top of page 93 aloud.

- Have students complete Exercise 1 individually. Walk around the classroom and help students as necessary.
- You may want to have students work with a partner to generate the subtopics.

Answers
1. Answers will vary. Possible answers:

Sports:
individual sports
sports played with one other person
team sports

Student life:
related to school
related to work
related to friends

Marriage:
the engagement period
the honeymoon
the first year of marriage

Fashion:
designers for women
designers for men
designers for children

Heroes:
in sports
in politics
in entertainment

Types of music:
classical
rock
rap

2

- Have students compare answers with a partner. If they generated the subtopics with a partner, have them compare in small groups.
- Go over answers as a whole class. Write some examples on the board.

Optional activity

Categories game
Have each student write a topic and three subtopics on an index card. Divide the class into two teams. Give each team the other team's set of cards. Students take turns choosing cards and reading the subtopics – but not the topics – to their team. If they guess the topic correctly, their team gets a point.

Lesson 4 — Be an architect!

page 94
Prewriting

1

- Read the instructions and question for Exercise 1 aloud.
- Call on a student to read the memo aloud.

2

- Read the instructions and question for Exercise 2 aloud.
- Call on students to read the list of items. Have students work individually to categorize the items: Say, *There may be some overlap in your choices.*

> **Answers**
> **2.** Answers will vary. Possible answers:
>   **a.** cafeteria, laundry room, sauna, showers, kitchen
>   **b.** computer room, garden, library, student lounge, copy center
>   **c.** game room, garden, gym, pool, pond, student lounge, tennis court

3

- Read the instructions for Exercise 3 aloud. Have students choose their favorite items with a partner.
- Ask, *What items would you most like to have in your dormitory?* Write several examples on the board.

> **Optional activity**
>
> **List expansion**
> Have students expand the lists from Lesson 4. Encourage them to be creative. Have them look at the sample poster on page 100 for ideas to add to their lists, such as indoor greenhouse, snack bar, rainwater showers, a running trail, *and so on.*

Lesson 5 — A floor plan for a new dormitory

page 95
Prewriting

- You may want to have students complete Lesson 5 as homework in preparation for the composition they will write in Lesson 6.
- Read the instructions aloud. Remind students of the guidelines in the memo from Lesson 4. Encourage them to use more than one color in their design.

- You may wish to refer students to the sample floor plan in Lesson 6. Give students the option of naming the rooms rather than drawing the icons.
- Tell students that the walls may be curved, the dorm may have multiple buildings, and there may be interior gardens as well.

Lesson 6 — Dormitory design

pages 96–97
Writing

1

- Read the instructions for Exercise 1 aloud.
- Ask, *Which place in the dorm would you most like to visit?*

2

- Read the instructions for Exercise 2 aloud.

- Have students read the composition individually.
- Then call on students to read the composition aloud, paragraph by paragraph.
- Have students work individually to complete a and b.
- Go over answers as a whole class.

<table>
<tr><td>

Answers

2. a. attention getter: Live Green!
main idea: This dorm has been specially
designed for students who enjoy being
surrounded by nature.
guide: We've included our Live Green
theme in facilities for daily living,
study, and recreation.

b. second paragraph: daily needs
third paragraph: studying
fourth paragraph: recreation

</td></tr>
</table>

3

- Read the instructions for Exercise 3 aloud.

- Have students write their composition on a
separate piece of lined paper, skipping lines.
Remind them to include their floor plan.

- Walk around the classroom, helping students as
necessary. You may want to have students
complete the composition as homework.

4

- Call on a student to read the Self-editing
checklist aloud.

- Give students about five minutes to review their
composition and complete the checklist.

| Lesson 7 | Using the articles *a, an,* and *the* |

page 98   **Editing**

- Call on a student to read the information and
examples at the top of page 98 aloud.

1

- Have students work individually or with a
partner to fill in the articles. Walk around the
classroom, helping students as necessary.
- Go over answers as a whole class.

<table>
<tr><td>

Answers

1. **b.** a	**k.** The
c. the	**l.** the
d. the	**m.** the
e. the	**n.** a
f. The	**o.** the
g. a	**p.** a
h. a	**q.** a
i. The	**r.** a
j. a	

</td></tr>
</table>

2

- Read the instructions for Exercise 2 aloud.
Allow students several minutes to review their
composition and complete the exercise.
- You may want to have students highlight any
changes they make.

Optional activity

More articles practice
*Find a paragraph at your students' reading level that
contains numerous articles. Retype the paragraph, omitting
the words a, an, and the. Have students fill in the missing
articles. Review the activity as a whole class.*

| Lesson 8 | What do you think? |

page 99   **Giving feedback**

1

- Read the instructions for Exercise 1 aloud.
- Divide the class into groups of four.

- Have students exchange their compositions with
students from another group, then complete a–c
independently.

2

■ Tell students to complete Exercise 2 when they have completed Exercise 1. Have them write their letter on a separate piece of lined paper.

3

■ Read the instructions for Exercise 3 aloud.

■ Have students spend 5–10 minutes discussing the compositions and awarding the ribbon. Say, *Be prepared to explain why you chose the design for the award.*

■ Discuss the exercise as a whole class. Call on the groups to present their favorite designs.

Option	Just for fun

page 100

1

■ Tell students that this is an exercise in which they can combine their writing and artistic skills to make a poster for their dorm.

■ Call on students to read the advertisement. Point out the features of the advertisement, such as an advertising slogan, a brief description, and contact information.

■ Have students complete their poster individually, either in class or at home.

■ You may want to have students work in pairs.

2

■ Collect the posters and display them around the classroom.

■ Have students walk around the classroom to look at the posters. Elicit reactions.

Unit 11 *My role models*

Overview

In this unit, students are asked first to discuss important people in their lives, and then to write a composition about one of those people. The composition includes a description of an experience the student had with this person, and an explanation of how the experience influenced the student's life.

This unit gives students practice in rearranging the paragraphs of their compositions to create different effects. The unit also introduces techniques for good paragraph transition and provides exercises on subject-verb agreement. Students will be given the opportunity to write a letter to the important person about whom they wrote in the final optional lesson.

	Lesson	Focus	Estimated Time
1	Important people in my life	Brainstorming	10–15 minutes
2	Linking paragraphs	Analyzing compositions	15–25 minutes
3	My two best friends	Analyzing compositions	20–25 minutes
4	An important person	Prewriting	20–25 minutes
5	Putting topics in order	Prewriting	20–30 minutes
6	An important person	Writing	50–60 minutes
7	Subject-verb agreement	Editing	15–20 minutes
8	What do you think?	Giving feedback	30–40 minutes
	Option: Just for fun		50–60 minutes

Key points

➤ Rather than presenting an expository writing mode, this unit concentrates on how ideas are sequenced in the overall composition.

➤ Make sure the students understand that being able to come up with a specific incident to write about is a key factor in deciding which person will be their subject.

➤ Maintain a positive classroom environment to encourage openness and self-disclosure.

➤ Sections can be skipped. A minimal set of lessons might include Lessons 4, 5, and 6. You can also save time by assigning some lessons as homework.

Important people in my life

page 101

Brainstorming

- Read the questions and instructions for Exercise 1 aloud.
- Have students brainstorm individually for three minutes to complete the list.
- Remind students that the people on their list should include both people they know personally and famous/important people they have never met.

- Walk around the classroom to encourage and help students as necessary.
- Elicit examples from individual students, and write them on the board.

2

- Read instructions for Exercise 2 aloud.
- Ask students to explain to their partner why those people influenced them. Remind them to give specific reasons and examples.

Lesson 2 **Linking paragraphs**

Analyzing compositions

page 102

- Call on students to read the information and examples at the top of page 102 aloud. Explain vocabulary as necessary.

1

- Read the instructions for Exercise 1 aloud. Have students work to complete the exercise individually.
- You may want to have students work with a partner to identify the links.

Answers
1. a. Transition
　b. Word
　c. Idea
　d. Transition

2

- Read the instructions for Exercise 2 aloud. Have students work with a partner to write linking sentences.
- Go over answers as a whole class. Write several student examples on the board.

Answers
2. Answers will vary. Possible answers:
Clint Eastwood usually plays the strong, silent type.
　In addition, Clint is always both cunning and charming in his films. (transition)

One of my favorite actors is Clint Eastwood.
　Eastwood is rugged, tough, and very good-looking. (word)

Clint Eastwood is probably best known for his westerns.
　Unforgiven has been called Clint's masterpiece. (idea)

Optional activity

Guessing game
Have students work in groups. Each student reads the sentences he or she wrote in Exercise 2 without saying the name of the famous person. The other students try to guess the famous person.

page 103

Analyzing compositions

1

2

▨ Read the instructions for Exercise 1 aloud.

▨ Have students read the composition individually. Allow several minutes, or enough time that the majority of the class seems to have finished reading.

▨ Call on students to read the composition aloud, sentence by sentence. Explain vocabulary as necessary.

▨ Ask students to underline the links connecting the paragraphs.

▨ Have students complete Exercise 2 individually.

Answers
2. Paragraphs 1–2: games (idea)
Paragraphs 2–3: pretending we're other people (words)
Paragraphs 3–4: another thing we like (idea)
Paragraphs 4–5: in conclusion (transition)

3

▨ Have students read the paragraph and go on to Exercise 4 individually.

4

▨ After students write their sentences, have them compare their answers with a partner.

▨ Elicit some examples from students and write them on the board.

Answers
4. Answers will vary. Possible answers:
Transition: First of all, Rose was an amazingly strong and determined woman.
Word: Rose was devoted to her family.
Idea: Her family was her greatest priority.

page 104

Prewriting

1

▨ Read the instructions for Exercise 1 aloud.

▨ Give students a few minutes to review their notes from Lesson 1 and fill in the information.

▨ Walk around the classroom to encourage and help students as necessary.

2

▨ Have students tell their partner about the person, relationship, and incident.

▨ Call on several students. Ask, *How did you choose? What was the incident?*

3

▨ Have students fill in the first box with additional information about the incident they chose. Walk around the classroom, helping students as necessary.

4

▨ Read the instructions for Exercise 4 aloud.

▨ Call on students to read the subtopics. Elicit other subtopics from the class.

▨ Have students fill in the remaining two boxes in Exercise 3.

Lesson 5 — Putting topics in order

page 105

Prewriting

1

- Read the instructions for Exercise 1 aloud. Call on students to read the two sample arrangements aloud, section by section.
- Ask the class which arrangement they prefer. Remind them there is no one correct answer.

2

- Read the instructions and questions for Exercise 2 aloud.
- Have students work individually on the arrangement of their composition by filling in the three possibilities in the boxes. Walk around the classroom, helping students as necessary.

3

- Have students discuss their arrangements with a partner.
- Ask students to decide which arrangement they like the best.

Optional activity

Storytelling
Have students tell their story to a partner in the arrangement they chose. Have them then change partners and tell the story again. This will help them refine the content.

Lesson 6 — An important person

page 106

Writing

1

- Read the instructions for Exercise 1 aloud.
- Have students read the composition individually.
- Call on students to read the composition aloud.
- Take some time to discuss this composition as a whole class. Ask students if they agree that we all must give things up throughout life. Call on individual students to express their opinions or share relevant experiences with the class.

2

- Read the instructions for Exercise 2 aloud. Tell students to write their composition on a separate piece of lined paper, skipping lines.
- You may want to assign this composition as homework.

3

- Call on a student to read the Self-editing checklist aloud.
- Give students about five minutes to review their composition and complete the checklist.

Optional activity

Show and tell
Have students bring in pictures of the person they wrote about and give a short presentation to their group. Tell them they should not read from their compositions, but should speak as naturally as they can. Encourage group members to ask questions.

Lesson 7 — Subject-verb agreement

page 107

Editing

- Call on a student to read the information and examples at the top of page 107 aloud.

1

- Read the instructions for Exercise 1 aloud.
- Have students work individually or with a partner to complete the exercise. Walk around the classroom, helping students as necessary.
- Go over answers as a whole class.

2

- Allow students several minutes to review their composition and correct any mistakes.
- You may want to have students highlight any changes they make.

| Lesson 8 | **What do you think?** |

Giving feedback

page 108

1

- Have students work in groups of four. Read the instructions for Exercise 1.
- Have each group exchange their four compositions with those of another group.

2

3

- Read the instructions for Exercises 2 and 3 aloud.
- Have students circle the expression that best describes the composition they just read. Tell them to then go on to Exercise 3.
- Walk around the classroom to encourage and help students as necessary.
- You may want to have students exchange the compositions they just read within their group, after they finish working on Exercise 3.

4

- Have students write their letter.
- You may choose to have students write their letter on a separate piece of lined paper. They can then give both the composition and letter back to the author.

Optional activity

More agreement practice
Have students write sentences about students in the class using each, every, neither, one of, someone, anything, everywhere, and nobody.

| Option | **Just for fun** |

page 109

1

- This is an enjoyable exercise that you may want students to complete on their own.
- Read the instructions for Exercise 1 aloud.
- Call on students to read the example letter, paragraph by paragraph.

2

- Have students write their letter.

3

- Give students the option of sending their letter.
- You can invite students to share their letter with their classmates, but students may want to keep their letter private.

Unit 12 Be a reporter

Overview

This final unit is more a finishing project than an instructional unit. The students study newspaper writing and write articles on local events. The articles are then collected, put into a newspaper or magazine format, and copied as a class newspaper for other students to read.

This unit teaches students to write headlines and identify different types of newspaper articles. The unit also introduces alternatives for the word *said*. In the final optional lesson, the students write a letter about the class to you, the classroom teacher. They also have the option of writing a letter about the textbook to us, the authors.

	Lesson	Focus	Estimated Time
1	In the news	Brainstorming	10–15 minutes
2	Writing for a newspaper	Analyzing writing style	15–25 minutes
3	Headlines	Learning about organization	20–25 minutes
4	Planning an article	Prewriting	20–25 minutes
5	A newspaper article	Writing	20–30 minutes
6	Other words for *said*	Editing	20–30 minutes
7	What do you think?	Giving feedback	20–30 minutes
8	Making a class newspaper	Desktop publishing	60–90 minutes
	Option: Just for fun		

Key points

➤ The class newspaper is an end-of-the-course culminating activity.

➤ Emphasize that although newspaper articles use different styles of writing, the basic style is simple, highly condensed, and non-evaluative.

➤ Concentrate on getting your students to understand the components of newspaper articles, as well as the different writing styles.

➤ To produce a publication that really looks like a newspaper, assess the students' computer skills beforehand and make reservations in a computer lab. If a computer is not available, have students type the articles and then "cut and paste" to make a newspaper.

➤ Consider different ways to distribute the final product.

➤ This unit may take more class time than the others, but sections can be skipped. The key writing lesson is Lesson 5.

In the news

page 110

Brainstorming

1

▓ Read the instructions for Exercise 1 aloud.

▓ Have a student read the examples in the list. Have students brainstorm individually for three minutes.

2

▓ Have students compare their lists with a partner and mark the most interesting topics.

3

▓ Elicit topics from the class and write them on the board.

▓ Encourage a variety of topics, including topics about school and community.

4

▓ Read the instructions for Exercise 4 aloud.

▓ Have students write the three topics that most interest them in their book.

▓ You may want to monitor students' topic choices to get a balanced set of articles for the newspaper.

Writing for a newspaper

page 111

Analyzing writing style

1

▓ Read the instructions for Exercise 1 aloud.

▓ Call on students to read the three explanations. Ask which ones they are most likely and least likely to read.

▓ You may want to elicit additional examples of other newspaper pages or sections. If possible, bring an English-language newspaper to class and have students look at it.

2

▓ Read the instructions for Exercise 2 aloud. Have students read the three articles individually.

▓ Call on students to read each article aloud. Instruct students to indicate on which page they might find these articles.

▓ Go over answers as a whole class.

Answers
2. a. Front page
   b. Society page
   c. Editorial page

3

▓ Discuss as a whole class which article is most interesting. Ask individual students to explain why.

Optional activity

Comparing and contrasting newspapers
Bring in or ask your students to bring in different kinds of newspapers. Have students work in groups to compare them. Ask students to find differences or similarities in layout, typeface, pictures, and content. You can find many newspapers on the Internet.

Learning about organization

page 112

I

▇ Read the instructions for Exercise 1 aloud.

▇ Call on students to read the names of the different sections. Explain vocabulary and article types if necessary. Ask students what the popular sections are.

2

▇ Have students complete the exercise individually. Remind them that there may be more than one answer.

▇ Go over answers as a whole class.

Answers
2. Answers will vary. Possible answers:

2. d	**8.** j
3. m	**9.** e
4. f	**10.** l
5. n	**11.** o
6. g	**12.** h
7. i	

3

▇ Give students several minutes to write their own headlines.

4

▇ Have students compare headlines with a partner.

▇ Elicit headlines from the class. Write several examples on the board.

▇ Ask students where in the newspaper the headlines would be found.

Optional activity

What's the headline?
Bring in copies of four to six short newspaper articles with the headline removed. Have students in groups write an appropriate headline for each article. Compare ideas as a whole class, then supply the actual headlines.

Prewriting

page 113

▇ Call on a student to read the suggestions at the top of the page aloud.

I

▇ Read the instructions for Exercise 1 aloud.

▇ Have students work individually to list three topics and styles. Remind them that they may use styles, such as surveys and reviews, that they practiced earlier in the course.

2

▇ Read the instructions for Exercise 2 aloud.

▇ Write several suggestions for topics on the board, and have students vote on the articles they would like to include.

▇ Have students decide as a whole class which article each student will write about.

3

▇ Have students complete the exercise with a partner. Walk around the classroom to encourage and help students as necessary.

pages 114–115

■ Have students read the article individually.

■ Call on students to read the article aloud.

■ You may want to assign roles to your students as they read aloud. Have one person role-play the narrator, one role-play Cindy, one her mother, and another her fiancé.

■ Have students complete a–e with a partner. Go over answers as a whole class.

Answers
a. human interest (from a small-town newspaper)
b. Who? Cindy Certello
What? returned home
When? last Thursday
Where? North Brookfield, Massachusetts
Why? to marry her high-school sweetheart

c. 5 fiancé's comments
2 changes
4 mother's comments
3 future plans

■ Have students complete d and e individually. Walk around the classroom, helping students as necessary.

■ Have students complete part f individually. You may want to examine these paragraphs before students finish their article.

■ Have students complete g. You may want to assign this as homework. If possible, have the students type their article.

page 116

1

■ Call on a student to read Exercise 1 aloud. Have students tell you what words in the article were used instead of *said*. Write the examples on the board.

Answers
1. exclaimed, commented, stated, cried, remarked, added

2

■ Read the instructions for Exercise 2 aloud. Call on students to read the columns of words.

■ Explain vocabulary as necessary. You may want to have students work with a partner to define the different words. Have student pairs or groups take turns explaining each column of words.

3

■ Read the instructions and questions for Exercise 3 aloud.

■ Have students work with a partner to complete the exercise.

■ Go over answers as a whole class.

■ Have students read the article individually and fill in the blanks, incorporating their new vocabulary.

Answers
3. speaking loudly: shout, scream, yell
speaking softly: mumble, whisper
Answers will vary. Possible answers:
Residents of Canton, Ohio, were surprised yesterday to find that City Hall had been painted yellow during the night. Mayor Joan Carter **exclaimed**, "We don't know who did it or how it happened. We are looking for the mysterious painter now. But," she **admitted**, laughing, "it's a nice color. I like it better than gray."
Not all of the town residents agree. Gavin Wang, a dentist, **complained**, "I think it's terrible. Whoever did this should be punished."

"Who did such a thing?" **cried** Barbara Koh, a grocery store owner. "No building is safe anymore," she **claimed**. "Where were the police?" she **demanded**.

Police officer Mark Morris **responded**, "We don't have any clues, but we're doing our best." He **mumbled** that he had a detective working on the case.

Hadas Bori, 6 years old, was very happy to see the brightly colored building on her way to school. "It's pretty!" she **shouted**. "I want someone to paint my school building the same color," she **added**.

4

- Read the instructions for Exercise 4 aloud.
- Give students several minutes to review their article. You may want to have students highlight any changes they make.

Lesson 7 What do you think?

page 117 — **Giving feedback**

1

- Divide the class into groups. Choose each group's members according to types of articles they wrote, if possible.
- Read the instructions for Exercise 1 aloud.
- Have students exchange articles within their group and complete a and b individually.

- You may want to give students a chance to rewrite their article based on the feedback.

2

3

- Have students read the rest of the articles.
- Tell the groups to try to agree on which article they like the best.

Lesson 8 Making a class newspaper

page 118 — **Desktop publishing**

- This group activity is an excellent way for students to learn about writing, computers, and journalism. It also gives you and your students a keepsake from the class.
- Divide students into groups according to areas of responsibility for the newspaper. One group can be responsible for proofreading or editing, another for typing, another for layout, another for artwork, another for type design and/or photos, etc.
- Call on students to read the suggestions at the top of page 118 aloud.

- Explain that serif fonts are typefaces that have little hooks on them, for example, Times or Courier. Sans serif fonts, such as Geneva and Helvetica, do not have hooks.

1

- Have students study the model layout.
- You may want to use an actual newspaper to make sure students understand the vocabulary.

2

- Have students work within their group to organize the newspaper.
- Allow enough time for this project. It may take several class sessions as well as outside work to complete.

Option	Just for fun

page 119

- Call on a student to read the instructions at the top of page 119 aloud.
- Have students write their evaluation individually and submit them to you.

- Encourage students to write to us, the authors. We would also enjoy hearing your feedback. Letters can be sent to:

Arlen Gargagliano
74 Lakeside Drive
New Rochelle, NY 10801

Curtis Kelly
Sunvale Sokokuji 2A
670-10 Sokokuji Monzen-cho
Kamigyo-ku, Kyoto 602-0898 Japan